The Understanding by Design
Guide to
Creating High-Quality Units

. . . . .

To Suzanne,
Your curriculum work
will transform Alexandria Public
Schools. Keep transfering the tasks!

Jay McTighe

**Other ASCD books
by Grant Wiggins and Jay McTighe**

Schooling by Design: Mission, Action, and Achievement
Understanding by Design Professional Development Workbook
Understanding by Design Expanded 2nd Edition

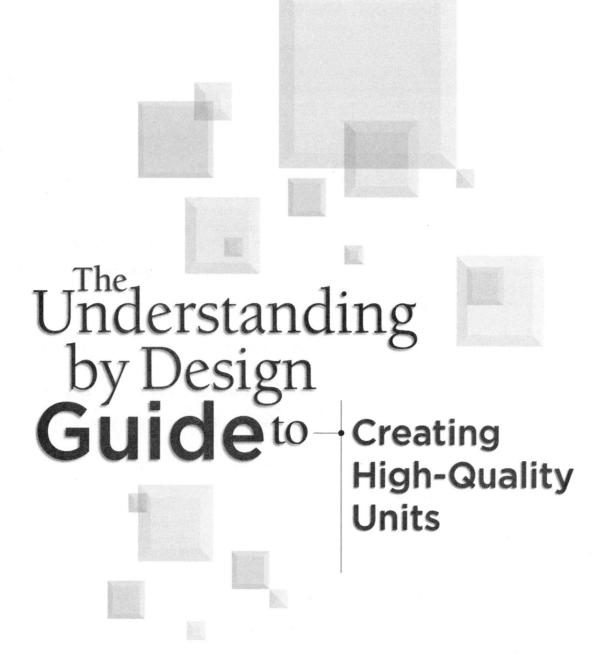

The Understanding by Design Guide to Creating High-Quality Units

GRANT WIGGINS AND JAY McTIGHE

Alexandria, Virginia USA

1703 N. Beauregard St. • Alexandria, VA 22311-1714 USA
Phone: 800-933-2723 or 703-578-9600 • Fax: 703-575-5400
Website: www.ascd.org • E-mail: member@ascd.org
Author guidelines: www.ascd.org/write

Gene R. Carter, *Executive Director;* Judy Zimny, *Chief Program Development Officer;* Nancy Modrak, *Publisher;* Scott Willis, *Director, Book Acquisitions & Development;* Julie Houtz, *Director, Book Editing & Production;* Darcie Russell, *Editor;* Georgia Park, *Senior Graphic Designer;* Mike Kalyan, *Production Manager;* Valerie Younkin, *Desktop Publishing Specialist;* Sarah Plumb, *Production Specialist*

All web links in this book are correct as of the publication date below but may have become inactive or otherwise modified since that time. If you notice a deactivated or changed link, please e-mail books@ascd.org with the words "Link Update" in the subject line. In your message, please specify the web link, the book title, and the page number on which the link appears.

PAPERBACK ISBN: 978-1-4166-1149-3   ASCD product 109107   n3/11

Also available as an e-book (see Books in Print for the ISBNs).

Quantity discounts for the paperback edition only: 10–49 copies, 10%; 50+ copies, 15%; for 1,000 or more copies, call 800-933-2723, ext. 5634, or 703-575-5634. For desk copies: member@ascd.org.

Library of Congress Cataloging-in-Publication Data
Wiggins, Grant P., 1950–
    The understanding by design guide to creating high-quality units / Grant Wiggins and Jay McTighe.
       p. cm.
    ISBN 978-1-4166-1149-3 (pbk. : alk. paper) 1. Curriculum planning—United States. 2. Curriculum-based assessment—United States. 3. Learning. 4. Comprehension. I. McTighe, Jay. II. Title.
    LB2806.15.W545 2011
    375'.001—dc22
                                                                            2010041160

21 20 19 18 17 16 15 14 13 12 11   1 2 3 4 5 6 7 8 9 10 11 12

The Understanding by Design Guide to
Creating High-Quality Units

· · · · ·

List of Figures

The figures critical to exploring Understanding by Design are printed within and page numbers are supplied. Additional figures that may be helpful are available online and are noted with the OO designation. All figures may be downloaded for your convenience.

Module G

Module H

Downloads/Key Page

The figures in this book, as well as additional worksheets and examples, are available for download at www.ascd.org/downloads

Enter this unique key code to unlock the files:

G1659 0E67D 0AB10

If you have difficulty accessing the files, e-mail webhelp@ascd.org or call 1-800-933-ASCD for assistance.

Introduction

The Understanding by Design Guide to Creating High-Quality Units is targeted to individuals and groups interested in improving their skills in designing units of study based on the Understanding by Design (UbD) framework. This guide introduces UbD unit design and directs readers through the process. It is organized around a set of modules that move from basic ideas (e.g., the three stages of "backward design") to more complicated elements of unit design (e.g., authentic performance tasks). Figure 1 shows a graphic representation of the organization of the modules.

Each module includes the following components:

- Narrative discussion of key ideas in the module
- Guiding exercises, worksheets, and design tips for unit design
- An example of an emerging design
- Review criteria (design standards) with prompts for self-assessment
- A list of resources for further information

Figure 1

Outline of Modules

Stage 1—Desired Results	Stage 2—Evidence	Stage 3—Learning Plan
Module A: The Big Ideas of UbD		
Module B: The UbD Template		
Module C: Starting Points		
Module D: Developing an Initial Unit Sketch		
Module E: Different Types of Learning Goals	Module F: Essential Questions and Understandings	Module G: Determining Evidence of Understanding and Developing Assessment Tasks
Module H: Learning for Understanding		

In addition to the print format, the *Guide to Creating High-Quality Units* features online resources correlated to the text. Many of the exercises and worksheets are accessible as downloads in electronic form, as are additional unit examples. The online portion includes frequently asked questions (FAQs) and will allow updates (e.g., more unit examples and new resources) to be readily accessed.

We invite users, especially beginners, to complete the exercises and worksheets to assist them in thinking through the unit design process. However, it is important to always keep the end—a coherent and well-aligned unit plan—in mind. If you find one or more exercises and worksheets unnecessary, feel free to skip them. Also, think of the exercises and worksheets as being like the training wheels on a bicycle. Eventually you'll find that you no longer need them as your understanding of UbD deepens and your unit design skills become more effective and automatic.

The modular presentation of this material means that users need not follow the modules in the order presented. As you can see from Figure 1, the volume is organized by the logic of the three stages of backward design. This logic should not be confused with a directive about the (inherently messy) process of design. Your interests, strengths, and prior experience as a designer will inevitably dictate how you use this book and the sequence you follow.

Think of this guide, then, as a cookbook. A cookbook has chapters devoted first to recipes for appetizers, then for soups and salads, then for fish and meat, vegetables, and desserts. Similarly, the *Guide to Creating High-Quality Units* is organized by the "menu" of a unit's parts—the elements of the unit template. But although the cookbook is organized, you need not read it from cover to cover or make all the recipes in the order in which they appear. So, too, in unit design. Like the recipe creator, you'll find that your path is informed by the need to put the final work in a certain form, but creation is inherently more nonlinear as you try things out, alter various "ingredients," and double-back to ensure that the end product works.

If you want more information on available products related to Understanding by Design, consult www.ascd.org. A community of people interested in UbD and additional resources are on ASCD EDge, accessible at http://groups.ascd.org/groups/detail/110884/understanding-by-design/. ASCD EDge is a professional networking community for educators.

Module A

The Big Ideas of UbD

Purpose: To become acquainted with the big ideas of Understanding by Design.

Desired Results: Unit designers will understand that

- Understanding by Design (UbD) is a curriculum-planning framework, not a prescriptive program.
- UbD focuses on helping students come to an understanding of important ideas and transfer their learning to new situations.
- UbD reflects current research on learning.

You should work on Module A if you are new to Understanding by Design.

You might skim or skip Module A if you are familiar with the basic ideas of UbD.

As its title suggests, *Understanding by Design* (UbD) reflects the convergence of two interdependent ideas: (1) research on learning and cognition that highlights the centrality of teaching and assessing for understanding, and (2) a helpful and time-honored process for curriculum writing (Wiggins & McTighe, 2005).

UbD is based on eight key tenets:

1. UbD is a way of thinking purposefully about curricular planning, *not* a rigid program or prescriptive recipe.

2. A primary goal of UbD is developing and deepening student understanding—the ability to make meaning of learning via "big ideas" and to transfer learning.

3. UbD unpacks and transforms content standards and mission-related goals into relevant Stage 1 elements and appropriate assessments in Stage 2.

4. Understanding is revealed when students autonomously make sense of and transfer their learning through authentic performance. Six facets of

understanding—the capacities to *explain, interpret, apply, shift perspective, empathize,* and *self-assess*—serve as indicators of understanding.

5. Effective curriculum is planned "backward" from long-term desired results through a three-stage design process (Desired Results, Evidence, Learning Plan). This process helps to avoid the twin problems of "textbook coverage" and "activity-oriented teaching" in which no clear priorities and purposes are apparent.

6. Teachers are coaches of understanding, not mere purveyors of content or activity. They focus on ensuring learning, not just teaching (and assuming that what was taught was learned); they always aim—and check—for successful meaning-making and transfer by the learner.

7. Regular reviews of units and curriculum against design standards enhance curricular quality and effectiveness.

8. UbD reflects a continuous-improvement approach to achievement. The results of our designs—student performance—inform needed adjustments in curriculum as well as instruction; we must stop, analyze, and adjust as needed, on a regular basis.

In this module, we'll explore two of the big ideas of UbD—*understanding* and *design*.

Understanding as an Educational Aim

The header for this section may strike readers as unnecessary. Don't all teachers want their students to understand what they teach? Perhaps. But an examination of many classrooms reveals that instruction is often focused on superficial coverage of lots of content as specified by national, state, or provincial standards, or as contained in distended textbooks. Even in nominally successful classrooms we see an overemphasis on short-term content acquisition for simple recall instead of long-term understanding. The teaching and learning process is also influenced in unfortunate ways by the pressure associated with high-stakes accountability tests. In many schools, teachers are expected to engage in "test prep" as a means of raising test scores. At its worst, this practice encourages and results in bad teaching—a low-level and formulaic approach to learning at the expense of exploring ideas in greater depth. Ironically, high-level achievement is actually undercut by such an approach (Wiggins, 2010).

Understanding by Design proposes a sound and commonsense alternative to these prevailing methods. UbD is predicated on the idea that long-term achievement gains are more likely when teachers teach for understanding of transferable concepts and processes while giving learners multiple opportunities to apply their learning in meaningful (i.e., authentic) contexts. The requisite knowledge and skills are learned and long recalled through the process of actively constructing meaning (i.e., coming to an understanding) and in transferring learning to new situations. In short, when we treat content mastery as the means, not the end, students learn more in the long term and can become more engaged in their work.

Support for an understanding-based approach to instruction and classroom assessment comes from research in cognitive psychology and neurology. The book *How People Learn: Brain, Mind, Experience, and School* (Bransford, Brown, & Cocking, 2000) provides a readable synthesis of the psychological research. Here are brief summaries of several key findings that provide a conceptual base for UbD's specific instruction and assessment practices:

- Effective learning requires not an exclusive focus on diligent drill and practice but rather a balanced focus on students' understanding and application of knowledge along with drill—much like what all good coaches do on the field or on the stage. Transfer requires learning strategy and alternate "moves" in all fields.

- To be widely applicable, learning must be guided by generalized principles. Knowledge learned at the level of rote memory rarely transfers; transfer most likely occurs when the learner understands underlying concepts and principles that can be applied to problems in new contexts. Learning with understanding is far more likely to promote transfer than simply memorizing information from a text or a lecture.

- Experts first seek to develop an understanding of problems or challenges, and this often involves thinking in terms of core concepts or big ideas (e.g., schemas, themes, models, theories, etc.). Novices' knowledge is much less likely to be organized around big ideas; novices are more likely to approach problems by searching for correct formulas and pat answers that fit their everyday intuitions.

- Research on expertise suggests that superficial coverage of many topics in the domain is a poor way to help students develop the competencies that will prepare them for future learning and work. Curricula that emphasize breadth of knowledge may prevent effective organization of knowledge because not enough time is provided to learn anything in depth. Curricula that are "a mile wide and an inch deep" risk developing disconnected rather than connected knowledge.

- Many assessments measure only recently taught knowledge and never ask for authentic performance (conditional knowledge and skill in context)—whether students know *when*, *where*, and *why* to use what they have learned in the past. This approach leads to surprisingly poor test results, because students do not recognize prior learning in unfamiliar-looking test questions—especially when the test has no context clues and hints (as occurs when teachers immediately quiz students on recent material.) Given that performance is the goal, local assessments typically do not provide a valid measure of student understanding.

Additional validation of the principles and practices of Understanding by Design comes from the emerging research on the neuroscience of learning (see, e.g., Willingham, 2009). Judy Willis (2006), a licensed neurologist and middle school teacher, notes the following instructional implications of this research:

- Patterning is the process whereby the brain perceives and generates patterns by relating new with previously learned material or chunking material into patterns it has not used before. Whenever new material is presented in such a way that students see relationships, they generate greater brain cell activity (forming new neural connections) and achieve more successful long-term memory storage and retrieval.
- Experiential learning that stimulates multiple senses in students, such as hands-on science activities, is not only the most engaging but also the most likely to be stored as long-term memories.
- The best-remembered information is learned through multiple and varied exposures followed by authentic use of the knowledge.

Research findings such as these provide a conceptual underpinning for Understanding by Design and should guide curriculum and assessment design, as well as instructional practice.

What *Is* Understanding?

The term *understanding* is surprisingly tricky, even though it is used widely. It has many different connotations. In fact, you may be aware that Benjamin Bloom and his colleagues (1956) avoided using the term in their taxonomy of the cognitive domain because it was seen as imprecise. Yet the term intuitively stands for something important—and different from content mastery, per se.

Therefore, at the start, we invite you to stop and reflect. *What is understanding? What do we mean when we say we want students to understand the content, not just know it? What's the difference between really "getting it" and just regurgitating back what was taught?*

If you are like most people, you identified a few clear yet different meanings of the term. Some of the meanings tend to be about ideas and inferences (e.g., making connections, seeing the big picture, grasping core concepts), and some tend to involve effective use of knowledge and skill (e.g., teach others, say it in your own words, apply learning to a real-world setting, defend your views to an audience). At this point, we merely note that the term is multifaceted, that understanding is something different from mere "knowing," and that the goal of understanding therefore involves more sophisticated instruction and assessment than teaching and testing for knowledge and skill alone. If the goal is understanding, *by design*, we'll need to plan mindful of these meanings.

Good Design = "Backward" Design

Teaching is a means to an end, and planning precedes teaching. The most successful teaching begins, therefore, with clarity about desired learning outcomes *and* about the evidence that will show that learning has occurred. Understanding by Design supports this view through a three-stage "backward-design" process used to plan curriculum units that include desired understandings and performance tasks that require transfer. Specific lessons are then developed in the context of a more comprehensive unit design.

The concept of planning curriculum backward from desired results is not new. In 1948, Ralph Tyler advocated this approach as an effective process for focusing instruction; Bloom's Taxonomy—and its recent revision by Anderson and Krathwohl (2001)—lays out the different types of educational aims and what they require of assessment; Robert Gagné (1977) and Robert Mager (1988) have long taught people how to analyze different outcomes and what they require of learning; more recently, William Spady (1994) popularized the idea of "designing down" from exit outcomes.

Although not a novel idea, backward design as we frame it results in more clearly defined and wisely blended short-term and long-term goals, more appropriate assessments, and more purposeful teaching than typical planning. This is particularly so if you acknowledge that a primary goal of education is effective transfer of learning. The key to UbD is to understand that, just like the coach or trainer, we must design backward from complex long-term performance where content is used, not from discrete topics or skills where content need only be recalled. Such performance lies at the heart of genuine expertise.

In other words, we want understanding *by design* as opposed to understanding by good fortune; that is, we don't want to just throw content and activities at the wall and hope something sticks. We need to think of unit design work as the intellectual equivalent of a GPS device in our car: by identifying a specific learning destination first, we are able to see the instructional path most likely to get us there.

This concept initially seems obvious. It turns out, however, to challenge many of our deepest habits as planners and teachers. Why? Because although we can easily say what we think should be taught and how we propose to teach it, the challenge we are proposing is different and more difficult. We don't start with content; we start with what students are expected to be able to do with content. What would real use of the content look like? What should students ultimately be able to say and do with content if they "get it"? And if that's what real learning looks like, what should be taught—and how—to make it most likely that the teaching leads to fluent, flexible, and lasting learning?

We trust you see that these are more difficult questions than initial impressions may have suggested. Note especially that this way of thinking backward from the desired changes in the student requires that we carefully think through what will count as evidence of real learning if we want to ensure that real learning is achieved and not just hoped for. Here, then, is a brief summary of the three stages of backward design used in UbD.

Stage 1—Identify Desired Results

- What long-term transfer goals are targeted?
- What meanings should students make to arrive at important understandings?
- What essential questions will students keep considering?
- What knowledge and skill will students acquire?
- What established goals/standards are targeted?

Stage 2—Determine Acceptable Evidence

- What performances and products will reveal evidence of meaning-making and transfer?
- By what criteria will performance be assessed, in light of Stage 1 desired results?
- What additional evidence will be collected for all Stage 1 desired results?
- Are the assessments aligned to all Stage 1 elements?

Stage 3—Plan Learning Experiences and Instruction Accordingly

- What activities, experiences, and lessons will lead to achievement of the desired results and success at the assessments?
- How will the learning plan help students achieve transfer, and meaning and acquisition, with increasing independence?
- How will progress be monitored?
- How will the unit be sequenced and differentiated to optimize achievement for all learners?
- Are the learning events in Stage 3 aligned with Stage 1 goals and Stage 2 assessments?

Figure A.1 is a graphic representation of the logic of backward design.

Avoiding the Twin Sins of Typical Unit Planning

We have found that when teachers follow this three-stage planning process—regardless of how much they use the full template described later in this *Guide to Creating High-Quality Units*—they are more likely to avoid the all-too-common "twin sins" of planning and teaching. The first sin occurs more widely at the elementary and middle school levels and may be labeled activity-oriented teaching. Here, teachers plan and conduct various activities, worrying only about whether they are engaging and kid-friendly. Unfortunately, this approach often confuses hands-on work with minds-on work. Too often, in other words, a collection of activities does not add up to coherent, focused, and generative learning. Haven't we all seen examples of classroom activities that don't meet these criteria? Such activities are like cotton candy—pleasant enough in the moment, but lacking long-term substance.

The second sin, more prevalent at the secondary and collegiate levels, goes by the name of content coverage. In this case, teaching consists of marching through a resource, be it a textbook or literature. With all due respect to the content-related challenges of secondary and college teaching, a teacher's job is not to simply mention everything in a book or on a topic; our job is to prioritize, make interesting and useful, and "uncover" the content, not merely "cover" it. The textbook should serve as a resource, not the syllabus, in a focused and effective learning plan. We have found that backward design is key to helping teachers in upper-level grades better understand their priorities, how to meet them, and how to use the textbook more judiciously to achieve worthy goals.

A Reflection on the Best Learning Designs

To further consider the qualities of good curriculum design and its effect on learning, we suggest that you reflect upon a few of the best-designed learning

Figure A.1

The Logic of Backward Design

Purpose: To illustrate and practice backward-design planning and thinking.

Directions: Sketch out a unit idea in the three stages of backward design. Use the driving example as a model. You might find it helpful to start with a simple nonacademic goal—for example, successfully "plan a trip" or "cook a meal."

Stage 1	Stage 2	Stage 3
If the desired end result is for learners to... →	**then you need evidence of the learners' ability to...** →	**then the learning events need to...**
Drive in heavy traffic with aggressive and inattentive drivers without accident or anger.	Handle real as well as simulated driving conditions in which defensive driving is required by traffic and behavior of other drivers.	Help novices become skilled in handling the automobile; help them learn and practice defensive driving in a variety of situations; help them learn to defuse anger using humor and different thought patterns, etc.

experiences you were ever involved in, and generalize from them. (If you are using this text in a class or study group, we suggest that participants reflect on, share and generalize from their experience in small groups, then as a whole group, using Figure A.5, available online.) *What was the best-designed learning you ever experienced? What is in general true of good design, regardless of the course content or the style of the teacher?* The answers we've heard most are captured in the list that follows. How does your list match up with these ideas? We bet there are quite a few matches, since effective designs for learning have common characteristics. We ask you to keep these qualities in mind as you begin your own unit design, and we'll remind you of them as you read and work.

Expectations. The best learning designs

- Provide clear learning goals and transparent expectations.
- Cast learning goals in terms of specific and meaningful performance.
- Frame the work around genuine issues/questions/problems.
- Show models or exemplars of expected performance and thinking.

Instruction. In the best learning designs

- The teacher serves as a facilitator/coach to support and guide learner inquiry.
- Targeted instruction and relevant resources are provided to equip students for expected performance.
- The textbook serves as one resource among many (i.e., text is resource, not syllabus).
- The teacher uncovers important ideas and processes by exploring essential questions and genuine applications of knowledge and skills.

Learning Activities. In the best learning designs

- Individual differences (e.g., learning styles, skill levels, interests) are accommodated through a variety of activities and methods.
- There is variety in work and methods; and students have some choice (e.g., opportunities for both group and individual work).
- Learning is active/experiential to help students make sense of complex content.
- Cycles of model-try-feedback-refine anchor the learning.

Assessment. In the best learning designs

- There is no mystery as to performance goals or standards.
- Diagnostic assessments check for prior knowledge, skill level, and misconceptions.
- Students demonstrate their understanding through real-world applications (i.e., genuine use of knowledge and skills, tangible product, target audience).

- Assessment methods are matched to achievement targets.
- Ongoing, timely, and descriptive feedback is provided.
- Learners have opportunities for trial and error, reflection, and revision.
- Self-assessment is expected and encouraged.

Sequence and Coherence. The best learning designs

- Start with a hook and immerse the learner in a genuine problem/issue/challenge.
- Move back and forth from whole to part, with increasing complexity.
- Scaffold learning in doable increments.
- Teach as needed; don't overteach all of the "basics" first.
- Revisit ideas—have learners rethink and revise earlier ideas or work.
- Are flexible (e.g., respond to student needs; are revised to achieve goals).

Note that such qualities are often missing from traditional activity-focused and coverage-focused teaching.

Design Standards

As responses to the exercise reveal, at the heart of the most effective learning are certain common conditions. Thus, curriculum and instructional designs should reflect and honor these conditions—that is, the conditions serve as guiding criteria for building our units. By using these general criteria (and others more specific to UbD, to be provided later), we can more purposefully review and improve our unit designs, our teaching, and student achievement.

In UbD we refer to such criteria as *design standards*. The standards reflect not only what we know from common sense but also what we know from the research about learning and best practice. It is thus wise to regularly engage in formal self-assessment and peer review of unit plans and overall curriculum designs. Such critical reviews of curricula are a centerpiece of UbD. By actively evaluating our work against established criteria, we make it far more likely that learners engage, learn, and achieve at high levels—that they understand by *design*, not by good luck.

Design standards specify the qualities that we strive for in our unit plans. Just as a writing rubric can inform students' compositions and guide them as they self-assess their drafts, the UbD standards function similarly for teachers. In fact, they have a dual purpose: (1) to guide self-assessment and peer reviews to identify design strengths and needed improvements; and (2) to provide a mechanism for quality control, a means of validating curricular designs. Because effective assessment should be ongoing, not simply an event at the end of a unit, you will see self-assessment questions related to these standards included in most of the modules of this *Guide*. (The UbD standards can be found in Module B.)

As you work through the *Guide to Creating High-Quality Units*, you may find it helpful to keep a running record or journal of your thoughts about the big ideas of UbD—understanding, transfer, effective design, teaching for understanding, backward design, and design standards. If you are using the guide in a study group or course, these questions and ideas will make for great discussions.

Go online to see Figure A.2 UbD in a Nutshell, which shows an overview of the key ideas of UbD and backward design as described in this module. Also online you'll find Figure A.3 What Is "Understanding"?, Figure A.4 What Is "Understanding" of Specific Topics?, Figure A.5 The Best Designs for Learning, and Figure A.6 Thinking About "Understanding."

Further Information on the Ideas and Issues in This Module

Understanding by Design, 2nd ed. (Wiggins & McTighe, 2005). The introduction provides an overview of Understanding by Design. Chapter 13 presents a more detailed summary of relevant research and addresses commonly voiced concerns.

Schooling by Design (Wiggins & McTighe, 2007). Chapter 1 discusses the mission of schooling, including a focus on understanding and transfer as fundamental educational goals. Chapter 4 presents a set of related learning principles that might guide professional actions and decisions.

"You *Can* Teach for Meaning" (McTighe, Seif, & Wiggins, 2004). This article provides a brief summary of research and the rationale for teaching understanding.

References

Anderson, L. W., & Krathwohl, D. (Eds.). (2001). *A taxonomy for learning, teaching and assessing: A revision of Bloom's taxonomy of educational objectives*. New York: Longman.

Bloom, B. (Ed.). (1956). *Taxonomy of educational objectives, handbook 1: Cognitive domain*. Chicago: University of Chicago Press.

Bransford, J., Brown, A., & Cocking, R. (Eds.). (2000). *How people learn: Brain, mind, experience, and school* (Expanded ed.). Washington, DC: National Academy Press.

Gagné, R. (1977). *Conditions of learning* (3rd ed.). New York: Holt, Rinehart, and Winston.

Mager, R. (1988). *Making instruction work or skillbloomers* (2nd ed.). Atlanta, GA: CEP Press.

McTighe, J., Seif, E., & Wiggins, G. (2004, September). You *can* teach for meaning. *Educational Leadership, 62*(1), 26–31.

Spady, W. (1994). *Outcome-based education: Critical issues and answers*. Arlington, VA: American Association of School Administrators.

Tyler, R. (1948). *Basic principles of curriculum and instruction*. Chicago: University of Chicago Press.

Wiggins, G. (2010, March). Why we should stop bashing state tests. *Educational Leadership, 67*(7), 48–52.

Wiggins, G., & McTighe, J. (2005). *Understanding by design* (2nd ed.). Alexandria, VA: ASCD.

Wiggins, G., & McTighe, J. (2007). *Schooling by design: Mission, action, and achievement*. Alexandria, VA: ASCD.

Willingham, D. T. (2009). *Why don't students like school?: A cognitive scientist answers questions about how the mind works and what it means for the classroom*. San Francisco: Jossey-Bass.

Willis, J. (2006). *Research-based strategies to ignite student learning*. Alexandria, VA: ASCD.

Module B

·························

The UbD Template

···

Purpose: To develop a preliminary understanding of the UbD Template, version 2.0, and to review sample UbD units in this format.

Desired Results: Unit designers will understand that

- The UbD Template is a tool that guides backward design and focuses a unit plan on the goal of understanding (as opposed to "coverage" or activities).

- Using the three-stage design process makes it more likely that unit goals, assessments, and instructional plans are coherent and aligned.

- Backward design is a way of thinking; it is not about filling in boxes in a template.

Unit designers will be able to

- Review existing units through the lens of the UbD Template.

- (Eventually) design units in the full UbD Template format.

You should work on Module B if you have not yet developed a unit using the UbD Template, version 2.0.

You might skim or skip Module B if you would prefer to work on Modules C and D to better understand the goal of "understanding" and how it differs from "knowing"; or if you wish to sketch a unit in broad-brush terms rather than work in the full-blown template just yet. In either case, you could then return to Module B.

···

The UbD Template, version 2.0, reflects the principles of sound curriculum, provides a helpful organizer for developing effective unit plans, and helps us avoid common weaknesses in unit designs. Like any new and powerful process, though, using the full-scale template may initially feel uncomfortable or unnecessarily complicated. You may want to start your design work in Module D in which you draft a unit in a simpler version of the template. However, many teachers have found that, with practice, it becomes a way of thinking—of clarifying learning goals and how to more likely achieve them—"by design."

Regardless of your style or interests as a designer, you will find it helpful to work through this module carefully to get the full picture of UbD and its potential to improve student learning. Figure B.1 presents the full UbD Template, version 2.0, with key questions for designers to consider.

Veterans of UbD will notice that this is a revised version of the familiar template. A summary of the changes to the template and the rationale for the changes can be found online in the Frequently Asked Questions section.

In this module we discuss each stage of the template in more detail. Examples of completed UbD unit designs are provided in the module. By reviewing these samples, you will develop a clearer sense of backward design, and get ideas to assist you with your own unit design.

Stage 1: Clarifying Desired Results

There are several major components to consider in Stage 1 when planning a UbD unit, reflective of the complexity of long-term academic objectives (see Figure B.1). Understanding is of course the key goal, and the template reflects this. Given our discussion of understanding in Module A, the boxes in Stage 1 should make sense. To "understand" has two general connotations: (1) applying your understandings, knowledge, and skill effectively in new situations results in successful transfer; and (2) making inferences and grasping connections, to culminate in understanding. We honor that distinction in the template: Understanding is separated into Transfer and Meaning; Meaning includes Understandings and Essential Questions.

Transfer

The ability to transfer is arguably the long-term aim of all education. You truly understand and excel when you can take what you have learned in one way or context and use it in another, on your own. The successful driver, soccer player, historian, or mathematician can size up a new challenge and transfer learning efficiently and effectively. Someone who learned only by rote cannot.

Meaning

An *understanding* is an idea that results from reflecting on and analyzing one's learning: an important generalization, a new insight, a useful realization that makes sense out of prior experience or learning that was either fragmented or puzzling. An understanding is not a fact (though it may sound like one) but a "theory" in the broadest sense; it is the result of inference—the developing and testing of ideas by learners, with teacher assistance, as needed—culminating in an idea that seems useful and illustrative to the learner.

For example, in our driving example shown later in this module, an understanding is that "The time needed to stop or react is deceptively brief, thus requiring constant anticipation and attention" (see Figure B.2). You only really "get" this idea from lots of experience and prompted reflection on that experience. Understandings are the hard-won ideas of modern expertise, whether they are about content or process, driving or physics. They can't be "covered"; they have to be "uncovered"—explored and considered—to be understood because they are not usually obvious and are prone to misunderstanding by novices. But more colloquially, you have to *own* the understanding. Otherwise it is just a lifeless sentence that you once heard in class, with no apparent value to you as you drive.

Transfer depends upon such meaning-making, then. We need vital and connective ideas to help us see themes/patterns/theories by which we can make sense of new otherwise-confusing situations. Deliberate anticipation of demands and likely trouble when we are driving helps us do more than prepare for novel challenges on the road. Careful forethought is more readily transferred as a habit of mind to other kinds of challenges requiring good anticipation, including those found in athletics and interpersonal situations.

Essential questions point us in the direction of both kinds of understanding. Coming to an understanding and applying prior learning requires an active process of meaning-making on the part of the learner. This process involves the ability to ask and pursue the most helpful questions, draw inferences, create new understandings, and actively process the effects of attempted transfer. The point of school is not merely to know things but to become better at and more assertive about inquiry. Powerful questions that frame all units signal this educational aim.

Essential questions are ongoing and guiding queries by which we make clear to students that true learning is about digging deeper; it is active, not passive. If we truly engage with a topic, we pursue questions that naturally arise: Why? How? What does this mean? What of it? What is its significance? What follows? These and other vital questions kindle our own meaning-making while helping us see the meaning and value of understandings developed by "experts."

The use of essential questions also facilitates transfer by pushing us to look for familiar patterns, connect ideas, and consider useful strategies when faced with novel challenges. A question is thus "essential" in an educational sense if it helps the learner achieve greater focus, understanding, and efficacy when dealing with new challenges. Ideally, an essential question that students initially explore eventually becomes their own and they use it to guide and organize all learning.

The first question in the driving example makes this clear: *What must I anticipate and do to minimize risk and accidents when I drive?* (see Figure B.2). Note, then, a fact about the template that you may not have considered: *Questions* are the desired result, not answers. The questions are not just setups for lessons. Learning to ask and pursue important questions on one's own is the desired result, and arguably key to all genuine lifelong learning.

Figure B.1

The UbD Template, Version 2.0

Stage 1—Desired Results

Established Goals		
What content standards and program- or mission-related goal(s) will this unit address?	**Transfer**	
	Students will be able to independently use their learning to . . .	
What habits of mind and cross-disciplinary goal(s)—for example, 21st century skills, core competencies—will this unit address?	What kinds of long-term independent accomplishments are desired?	
	Meaning	
	UNDERSTANDINGS *Students will understand that . . .*	ESSENTIAL QUESTIONS *Students will keep considering . . .*
	What specifically do you want students to understand? What inferences should they make?	What thought-provoking questions will foster inquiry, meaning-making, and transfer?
	Acquisition	
	Students will know . . .	*Students will be skilled at . . .*
	What facts and basic concepts should students know and be able to recall?	What discrete skills and processes should students be able to use?

Figure B.1

The UbD Template, Version 2.0 *(continued)*

Stage 2 — Evidence

Code	Evaluative Criteria	
Are all desired results being appropriately assessed?	What criteria will be used in each assessment to evaluate attainment of the desired results?	**PERFORMANCE TASK(S):** *Students will show that they really understand by evidence of …* How will students demonstrate their understanding (meaning-making and transfer) through complex performance?
	Regardless of the format of the assessment, what qualities are most important?	**OTHER EVIDENCE:** *Students will show they have achieved Stage 1 goals by …* What other evidence will you collect to determine whether Stage 1 goals were achieved?

Stage 3 — Learning Plan

Code		
	What pre-assessments will you use to check student's prior knowledge, skill levels, and potential misconceptions?	*Pre-Assessment*
What's the goal for (or type of) each learning event?	**Learning Events** *Student success at transfer, meaning, and acquisition depends upon …* • Are all three types of goals (acquisition, meaning, and transfer) addressed in the learning plan? • Does the learning plan reflect principles of learning and best practices? • Is there tight alignment with Stages 1 and 2? • Is the plan likely to be engaging and effective for all students?	*Progress Monitoring* • How will you monitor students' progress toward acquisition, meaning, and transfer, during lesson events? • What are potential rough spots and student misunderstandings? • How will students get the feedback they need?

Figure B.2

Driver's Education Unit

Stage 1—Desired Results

Established Goals	Transfer
Drive the vehicle safely and responsibly.	*Students will be able to independently use their learning to …*
Negotiate the road correctly.	T1 Drive courteously and defensively without accidents or needless risk.
Comply with signals, signs and road markings.	T2 Anticipate and adapt their knowledge of safe and defensive driving to various traffic, road, and weather conditions.

Meaning

	UNDERSTANDINGS	ESSENTIAL QUESTIONS
Interact appropriately with other road users.	*Students will understand that …*	*Students will keep considering …*
Minimize risk when driving.	U1 Defensive driving assumes that other drivers are not attentive and that they might make sudden or ill-advised moves.	Q1 What must I anticipate and do to minimize risk and accidents when I drive?
Learn from experience.	U2 The time needed to stop or react is deceptively brief, thus requiring constant anticipation and attention.	Q2 What makes a courteous and defensive driver?
	U3 Effective drivers constantly adapt to the various traffic, road, and weather conditions.	

Acquisition

Students will know …	Students will be skilled at …
K1 The driving laws of their state, province, or country.	S1 Procedures of safe driving under varied traffic, road, and weather conditions.
K2 Rules of the road for legal, courteous, and defensive driving.	S2 Signaling/communicating intentions.
K3 Basic car features, functions, and maintenance requirements (oil changes, etc.).	S3 Quick response to surprises.
	S4 Parallel parking.

Source: Goals adapted from the Driving Standards Agency, United Kingdom. © Crown Copyright 2010. www.dsa.gov.uk.

Figure B.2

Driver's Education Unit *(continued)*

Code	Evaluative Criteria	Stage 2—Evidence
All Transfer Goals	• Skillful • Courteous • Defensive	PERFORMANCE TASK(S): *Students will show that they really understand by evidence of …* Their ability to transfer all their discrete learning into real-world (or simulated) responsive, safe, and courteous driving, under varied conditions. For example,
All Meaning Goals	• Anticipates well • Responsive to varied road conditions	1. *Task:* Drive from home to school and back, with parental and teacher supervision. The goal is to demonstrate skillful, responsive, and defensive driving under real-world conditions. 2. *Task:* Same task as 1, but with rainy conditions. 3. *Task:* Same task as 1, but in rush-hour traffic. 4. *Booklet:* Driving for newbies. Write a booklet for other young drivers on the do's and don'ts of safe and effective driving.
All Meaning Goals	• Proficient in driving skills • Knowledge-able (driving-related laws, traffic signs and symbols, basic car parts, etc.)	OTHER EVIDENCE: *Students will show they have achieved Stage 1 goals by …* 5. Self-assessing driving and parking in Tasks 1–3, in terms of courteous and defensive. Discuss adjustments made. 6. Showing evidence of discrete skills as well as overall fluency in a driving simulator and off road.
All Skill and Transfer Goals		7. Identifying driver errors in video clips, without prompting by teacher. 8. Quiz on basic car parts, functions, and necessary maintenance.
All Knowledge and Skills Goals; simple transfer		9. Passing the written test as a measure of knowing the rules of the road and applicable laws, passing the road test as an indicator of meeting all Stage 1 skill and transfer goals.

Figure B.2

Driver's Education Unit *(continued)*

Code		Stage 3—Learning Plan		
	•	Pre-assessment of driving knowledge, skill, understandings, and attitudes using surveys and simulators	*Pre-Assessment*	*Progress Monitoring*

Learning Events

T

Student success at transfer, meaning, and acquisition depends upon . . .

Applying their learning, first off-road, then on-road. All instruction is carried out and formatively assessed under a five-level system of increased autonomy:

• The skill is introduced.
• The skill can be carried out under full instruction.
• The skill can be carried out correctly only when prompted.
• The skill can be carried out correctly with occasional prompting.
• The skill can be carried out consistently without any prompting.

M

Interpreting road conditions and the status of the automobile. Reflection and generalizations are promoted via discussion of the essential questions after each virtual and real-road experience. Written self-assessment is required after each driving experience. Expert driving is modeled via video and the driving instructor, and the driver generalizes about good (vs. poor) driving.

A

Learning the key skills of driving, the rules of the road, and basic car facts. Experience and equipping via direct instruction and video simulators are provided, including how to handle wet roads, dry roads, darkness, daylight, highway, city, country. Instruction on key laws and rules of the road, and practice tests are used.

Separate skill development and real-world practice in

Car Check	Circles	Safety Checks	Pedestrian Crossings
Controls and Instruments	Highways	Starting Up, Moving, and Stopping	Turns
Safe Positioning	Reversing	Mirrors	Parking
Signals	Emergency Stopping	Anticipation and Planning Ahead	Darkness
Use of Speed	Weather Conditions	Other Traffic	Rules and Laws
Intersections	Security	Passengers	Loads

Pre-Assessment *(empty)*

Progress Monitoring

• Formative assessment and informal feedback by instructor as student tries to apply skills learned while driving off-road.

• Look for common misconceptions and skill deficits, including

  ○ Failure to check mirrors and peripheral vision.

  ○ Inaccurate responses to changing road conditions.

  ○ Failure to accurately perceive speed of other cars during merges and turns.

Source: Skills modified from the Driving Standards Agency, United Kingdom. © Crown Copyright 2010. www.dsa.gov.uk.

Module E goes into further detail about the goals of transfer, meaning, knowledge, and skill. Module F goes into greater detail on essential questions and understandings and how to craft them. Module H goes into more depth about how to work with ideas instructionally.

Acquisition

In the short term, our aim is that students acquire *knowledge* and *skill*. Knowledge and skill goals are familiar to all readers of this guide. Here, you state the key declarative knowledge (factual information, vocabulary, and basic concepts) and procedural knowledge (basic know-how or discrete skills) you want your students to learn by the unit's end.

In UbD, we consider the knowledge and skill as the necessary tools (i.e., the *means*) of thoughtful and effective performance, and they must be taught and assessed as such—just as they are currently taught and assessed in sports and the professions (i.e., drills are necessary but not sufficient). The ultimate bottom-line goal (i.e., the *end*) of learning "content" is successful meaning and transfer of prior learning to new situations. The UbD Template reflects this view of schooling.

The challenge here is not so much to identify all possible relevant knowledge and skill goals but rather to winnow the list down to the essentials. By "the essentials" we mean three things:

- *The knowledge and skill that are core building blocks for later meaning-making and transfer.* We need to avoid just listing picayune facts or definitions that do not contribute to understanding.
- *You plan to assess whether students have the targeted knowledge and skill.* Only place in Stage 1 what you intend to explicitly assess and teach, not what just gets mentioned.
- *The targeted knowledge and skill fit naturally within this unit.* Learning them will not seem disconnected or arbitrary to the students in the context of the unit as a whole.

Design Tip: Some people find it helpful to state the knowledge goals as recall questions that students should be able to answer on their own by the unit's end. This has a double benefit: it helps you distinguish the essential questions from the factual questions, and it tends to shorten the list of knowledge objectives. Additionally, this suggests what the assessments in Other Evidence in Stage 2 need to accomplish.

Standards and Other Established Goals

Many users of this guide are obligated to address externally mandated standards (national, state, provincial or district) and district or school goals (e.g., mission statements, 21st century skills, habits of mind) when they design curriculum and unit plans. So, there is a specific box for such Established Goals on the template, on the left-hand side of Stage 1. This is where you should list relevant state or provincial standards as well as formal course or program goals. School or district mission-related goals related to the unit topic should also be noted here.

We have placed these mandated goals on the side to remind educators that while the standards are important to consider in unit design work, they are not usually the purpose of schooling. As we argue in greater detail later, standards are like the building code in construction: they have to be met, but they do not reflect the ultimate aim of any design, nor do they encompass everything that matters to the design's users.

A further reason for putting the Established Goals box on the side is that most state standards involve multiple layers of different learning goals. For example, in the new Common Core Standards for Reading, a standard under the strand Key Ideas and Details reads, "Determine a central idea of a text and how it is conveyed through particular details; provide a summary of the text distinct from personal opinions or judgments" (adapted from *Common Core State Standards Initiative* 2010, 6th Grade Standards, p. 36). This one standard implicitly contains many UbD elements: understandings about main idea and summarizing, varied skills and strategies, and the transfer goal of finding main ideas in a new text on your own. Figure B. 3 provides a graphic example of this kind of "unpacking" of an established goal to show how unit designers need to proceed. (Failure to do this kind of unpacking is a common source of weak local curriculum and assessment.)

In short, the Stage 1 elements should be thought of as interconnected, not independent and isolated. The visual shape of the template in Stage 1 is meant to remind teacher-designers that the standards are necessary but not sufficient, that knowledge and skill are means to understanding ends, and that the essential question(s) are central to any work focused on meaning-making and transfer.

Take a look back at Figure B.2, Stage 1, in the driver's education curriculum. Notice how the various elements work together to help define the goals of the design.

Stage 2: Determining Needed Evidence

In Stage 2, teachers must carefully "think like an assessor" to consider the evidence needed to determine the extent to which students have achieved the identified knowledge, skills, and understandings in Stage 1. Indeed, the essence of backward design is to logically tease out what the goals (identified in Stage 1) imply for the assessments (Stage 2), and then instruction (Stage 3). The UbD Template embodies this logic. Refer back to Figure B.1 to see an overview of Stage 2.

If you engaged in the "What Is 'Understanding'?" exercise online (figures A.3 and A.4), you already have a sense of the kinds of evidence that signify understanding or lack of it. In general, we can say that if learners really understand something, they can effectively apply and explain in some performance. By "performance" we do not mean a mechanical, scripted response or mindless plugging in of a

Figure B.3

Unpacking Standards for Stage 1

Stage 1—Desired Results		
Established Goals	**Transfer**	
Common Core English Standards (Reading) *Key Ideas and Details* 1. Cite textual evidence to support analysis of what the text says explicitly as well as inferences drawn from the text. 2. Determine a central idea of a text and how it is conveyed through particular details; provide a summary of the text distinct from personal opinions or judgments. 8. Trace and evaluate the argument and specific claims in a text, distinguishing claims that are supported by reasons and evidence from claims that are not.	*Students will be able to independently use their learning to . . .* • Cite textual evidence (and inferences drawn from the text), with no teacher prompting or scaffold, to support an analysis of what a newly encountered nonfiction text says. • Determine a central idea of a text and provide a neutral summary, without evaluation, of it; then, evaluate it.	
	Meaning	
	UNDERSTANDINGS *Students will understand that . . .* • The text presents an argument, not just facts and opinions. • The reader's first job is to follow the argument; then, you can critique it. • Key aspects of the argument may only be implied and thus need to be inferred.	ESSENTIAL QUESTIONS *Students will keep considering . . .* • What's the author's point? How does he support it? How valid is the support? • How would I best summarize the text? • Do I agree with the author?
	Acquisition	
	Students will know . . . • The text well enough to provide an accurate retelling of what the text says. • Key vocabulary in the text. • The elements of a valid argument.	*Students will be skilled at . . .* Providing a neutral summary. • Tracing the logic of an argument. • Evaluating the strength of an argument in a text. • Using reading strategies to identify main ideas and author purpose.

memorized formula. Rather, we expect students to flexibly and intelligently use what they know, in a new complex situation where higher-order thinking in the use of content is required. When we speak of "explanation," we seek more than a memorized recitation. We expect learners to put it in their own words, give reasons based on evidence for their answers, cite a text to support their position, show their work, justify their solution, and so on. Thus, when assessing for understanding there usually needs to be at least one such task, as the Stage 2 part of the template makes clear. (Later in this book we will propose a more nuanced conception involving six facets of understanding. For now, we want to keep it simple.)

Assessments of understanding ask teachers to select or develop tasks that require students to demonstrate the degree to which they achieved the understanding identified in the Transfer and Meaning boxes in Stage 1. Since such assessments are typically open-ended (i.e., they generally do not have a single or final correct answer or approach), we need evaluative criteria to judge student responses. These criteria are placed in front of the specific assessments on the template (and are eventually turned into more detailed rubrics before teaching). Why place the criteria first? Because the criteria link the specific tasks back to the (more general) Desired Results of Stage 1. See, for example, how this works in the driving example: the criteria—skillful, courteous, defensive, anticipates well—apply to *all* would-be performance tasks related to driving; they explicitly link back to the language of the transfer goals and other desired results.

Under the space for listing performance tasks in Stage 2, other assessments of a more traditional kind are listed below, where it says Other Evidence. Here, you place assessments of knowledge, skill, standards, and other goals that are not otherwise assessed by the performance tasks. For example, if you want to see if students *know* multiplication tables or world capitals, then you might use familiar objective test items, such as multiple-choice, matching, short-answer, true-false, or fill-in-the-blank, to provide the needed evidence in an efficient manner. Similarly, you can assess for discrete proficiency of *skill* by using a skill check or simple demonstration. Or, you might call for an essay on one or more essential questions to gauge whether students have achieved the understandings. But don't just list the format here: first, summarize *what evidence* the assessments will provide (e.g., "quiz providing evidence that the student can recall number facts and solve simple problems of subtraction").

It is important to understand that isolated or discrete tests of knowledge and skill can never be the most important summative evidence of meeting the higher-order and long-term Stage 1 goals. The long-term goal of learning is transfer, not cued response to test questions. Like the drills in soccer or the five-paragraph essay in writing, most test items are simplified *means* to achievement of transfer, not the *end*. They are *necessary* but *not sufficient evidence* of genuine competence.

Let's return to the driver's education example and have a look at a completed Stage 2 template in Figure B.2. Because the end goal is effective driving on real roads, we need assessments that involve real or simulated road conditions (above and beyond the paper-and-pencil test and isolated exercises on specific skills, in Other Evidence). The example thus illustrates a key point about all assessment and backward design: To allow valid inferences to be drawn from the results, an assessment must always provide an appropriate measure of a given goal. It cannot just be any old performance. It has to be a performance that can only be done well by learners who "get it." This is what we mean in education when we ask "Is this a valid assessment?" What we really mean is "Will the results from this assessment enable us to conclude with confidence whether our Stage 1 goals were achieved?" (Validity is further discussed in Module F.)

This is the point of the column in Stage 2 (and Stage 3) on the far left entitled "Code." Whether you simply put check marks, the code of T, M, or A (for transfer, meaning, acquisition), or more elaborate coding (e.g., T1, M2, EQ2 by which you note the specific Stage 1 elements being assessed by the assessment), the coding column will encourage you to be self-disciplined about ensuring that your assessments reflect your goals and that all goals are covered by the proposed assessments.

Stage 3: Developing the Learning Plan

In Stage 3 we plan for the most appropriate learning experiences and needed instruction. The logic of backward design mandates that our learning plan aligns with our goals (Stage 1) and their corresponding assessments (Stage 2). The template signals this by the first column in Stage 3 as in Stage 2; that is, we make a deliberate effort to check that our proposed learning events honor our goals and learning principles. This helps us avoid the aforementioned "twin sins" of mere coverage and activity-oriented teaching. Refer to Figure B.2 to see Stage 3 for the driver's education example.

Note, too, that there is room provided at the top and side of Stage 3 for formative assessment in the broadest sense: pre-assessments before the unit begins, and ongoing progress monitoring on the right side. The research is clear and supports common sense: a good unit is not a rigid plan but a flexible framework in which we are always prepared to adjust based on feedback. To put it paradoxically, in the best designs we *plan* to be responsive; we plan to adjust. Far too many lesson, unit, and course designs are too rigid—unresponsive to student confusion, skill deficits, or misunderstandings. (This problem is exacerbated by pacing guides that focus only on teaching to a rigid schedule instead of guides that help you achieve goals despite unexpected detours.) Stage 3 in its new form encourages designers to think through the likely trouble spots and how to monitor and adjust for them in the unit *before* it's too late.

You may have wondered why diagnostic and formative assessments are not placed in Stage 2. The reason has to do with the aim of such information: unlike the summative evidence asked for in Stage 2, the point of pre-assessments and ongoing monitoring is to advance learning. We think it is therefore more sensible to place this part of the design in Stage 3.

In drafting a unit, the learning plan need not be developed into full-blown lesson plans with all details mapped out. The key in unit design is to see the bigger picture of which kinds of learning events are needed to achieve the desired results specified in Stage 1. Then, your daily lessons can be fleshed out with the confidence that they will reflect your longer-term and most important goals. The sample units you will find later in this module reflect this: the Stage 3 examples summarize learning events related to the three different kinds of goals in Stage 1. From this summary of valid options, the final task of developing a detailed and sequenced lesson plan can occur with greater confidence about the alignment of the plan to the goals and assessments. (In the online materials we provide a few examples of full-blown lesson plans for some of the examples provided below.)

The Design Standards

As we noted in Module A, there is a set of design standards for self-assessment and peer review of work in the unit template. The standards summarize the points made thus far about the template and its demands. If you develop the discipline of checking against these standards a few times before declaring the unit done, your work is far more likely to be excellent than if you just draft something in one pass. An author doesn't just write from the introduction to the end. There is a constant back-and-forth to ensure that the writing reflects purpose and the integrity of the story. Regular analysis of the whole unit via the design standards can help you develop that habit. See Figure B.4 for the Unit Design Standards.

Before-and-After Examples

A useful teaching technique for developing understanding involves presenting learners with examples and nonexamples of a concept, principle, or process. By analyzing and comparing the distinguishing features of the examples contrasted with the nonexamples, learners deepen their understanding of key ideas. This same process will work for you, the reader, not just for your students. Accordingly, we offer the following "before-and-after" examples, with brief comments, to help you better understand the value of the template and the weaknesses of many typical units of study.

In the Social Studies Unit Before UbD example, Figure B.5, we see a collection of activities without clear purpose or organizing ideas. A "before UbD" algebra example (provided online as Figure B.7) reflects a similar problem with a

Figure B.4

Unit Design Standards

Key: 3 = Meets the standard; 2 = Partially meets the standard; 1 = Does not yet meet the standard

Stage 1	3	2	1	Feedback and Guidance
1. The listed transfer goals specify desired long-term, genuine accomplishment.				
2. The identified understandings reflect important, transferable ideas.				
3. The identified understandings are stated as full-sentence generalizations—"Students will understand that…."				
4. Essential questions are open-ended and thought provoking.				
5. Relevant standards, mission, or program goals are addressed explicitly in all three stages.				
6. The identified knowledge and skill are needed to address the established goals, achieve the targeted understanding(s), and support effective transfer.				
7. All the elements are aligned so that Stage 1 is focused and coherent.				
Stage 2				
8. The specified assessments provide valid evidence of all desired results; that is, Stage 2 aligns with Stage 1.				
9. The specified assessments include authentic transfer tasks based on one or more facets of understanding.				
10. The specified assessments provide sufficient opportunities for students to reveal their attainment of the Stage 1 goals.				
11. Evaluative criteria for each assessment are aligned to desired results.				
Stage 3				
12. Appropriate learning events and instruction will help learners				
a. Acquire targeted knowledge and skills. b. Make meaning of important ideas. c. Transfer their learning to new situations.				
13. The WHERETO elements are included so that the unit is likely to be engaging and effective for all learners. (See Figure A.2 online for explanation of WHERETO.)				
Overall				
14. All three stages are coherent and in alignment.				
15. The unit design is feasible and appropriate for this situation.				

different cause—the unit simply reflects a march through a textbook and its topics. The Social Studies Unit (after UbD), shown as Figure B.6, and the Algebra Unit (after UbD), shown as Figure B.8 (online), provide a more intellectually challenging, focused, and coherent learning experiences. Instead of activities strung together loosely around a topic, there is now a clear focus on important ideas and questions, tighter alignment between the unit goals and assessments, and more purposeful and engaging learning activities in Stage 3.

Sample Units

We invite you to study brief examples of other units designed in multiple-page versions of the UbD Template. Once again, feel free to record ideas for your unit in any box of a blank template, with the understanding that we will be explaining each element in much more detail as you proceed through the modules in this book. These sample units are available online and as downloads for your consideration.

Figure B.5

Social Studies Unit Before UbD

Topic
Topic: Westward Movement and Pioneer Life Social Studies—3rd Grade
Activities
1. Read textbook section—"Life on the Prairie." Answer the end-of-chapter questions.
2. Read and discuss *Sarah Plain and Tall*. Complete a word-search puzzle of pioneer vocabulary terms from the story.
3. Create a pioneer-life memory box with artifacts that reflect what life might be like for a child traveling west or living on the prairie.

4. Prairie Day activities—Dress in pioneer clothes and complete seven learning stations:
   a. Churn butter
   b. Play 19th century game
   c. Send letter home with sealing wax
   d. Play "dress the pioneer" computer game
   e. Make a corn-husk doll
   f. Try quilting
   g. Do tin punching

Assessments
1. Quiz on pioneer vocabulary terms from *Sarah Plain and Tall*
2. Answers to end-of-chapter questions on pioneer life
3. Show-and-tell for memory box contents
4. Completion of seven learning stations during Prairie Day
5. Student reflections on the unit

Figure B.6

Social Studies Unit

Stage 1—Desired Results		
Established Goals	**Transfer**	
Students pose relevant questions about events they encounter in historical documents, eyewitness accounts, oral histories, letters, diaries, artifacts, photographs, maps, artworks, and architecture.

Trace why their community was established, how individuals and families contributed to its founding and development, and how the community has changed over time, drawing on maps, photographs, oral histories, letters, newspapers, and other primary sources. | *Students will be able to independently use their learning to . . .*

• Seek out, compare, and critique different historical accounts.
• Compare the lives of pioneers on the prairie and "pioneers" today, on their own.
• View interactions of civilizations, cultures, and peoples with greater perspective and empathy. | |
| | **Meaning** | |
| | UNDERSTANDINGS
Students will understand that . . .

• Many pioneers had naïve ideas about the opportunities and difficulties of moving west.
• People move for a variety of reasons—for new economic opportunities, greater freedoms, or to flee something.
• Successful pioneers rely on courage, ingenuity, and collaboration to overcome hardships and challenges.
• The settlement of the west threatened the lifestyle and culture of Native American tribes living on the plains.
• History involves making sense of different "stories." | ESSENTIAL QUESTIONS
Students will keep considering . . .

• Why do people move? Why did the pioneers leave their homes to head west?
• How do geography and topography affect travel and settlement?
• What is a pioneer? What is "pioneer spirit"?
• Why did some pioneers survive and prosper while others did not?
• Whose story is it?
• What happens when cultures interact? |
| | **Acquisition of Knowledge and Skill** | |
| | *Students will know . . .*

• Key facts about the westward movement and pioneer life on the prairie.
• Pioneer vocabulary terms.
• Basic geography (travel routes of pioneers and location of their settlements).
• Key factual information about Native American tribes living on the plains and their interactions with the settlers. | *Students will be skilled at . . .*

• Using research skills (with guidance) to find out about life on the wagon train and prairie.
• Expressing their findings orally and in writing. |

Figure B.6

Social Studies Unit (*continued*)

Evaluative Criteria	Stage 2—Evidence
	Students will show their learning by...
• Historically accurate	PERFORMANCE TASK(S):
• Well crafted	Evidence is needed of student ability to generalize from the pioneer experience. Ideas:
• Revealing and informative	• Create a museum display, including artifacts, pictures, and diary entries, depicting "a week in the life" of a family of settlers living on the prairie. (What common misunderstandings do folks today have about prairie life and westward settlement?) Explain how geography and topography affected pioneer travels and settlement.
• Good detail	• Write 1 letter a day (each representing a month of travel) to a friend back east, describing your life on the wagon train and the prairie. Tell about your hopes and dreams, then explain what life on the frontier was really like. (Students may also draw pictures and explain orally.)
• Clear explanation	• Formal oral presentation to teacher, parent, or aide: museum docent speech at an exhibit of 19th, 20th, and 21st century pioneers. How are we pioneers? How are modern pioneers like and unlike the people on the prairie?
• Mechanically sound	• Imagine that you are an elderly tribal member who has witnessed the settlement of the plains by the pioneers. Tell a story to your 8-year-old granddaughter about the impact of the settlers on your life. (This task may be done orally or in writing.)
• Well argued	OTHER EVIDENCE:
	• Oral and/or written response to one of the essential questions, using pioneer vocabulary in context.
	• Drawing(s) showing hardships of pioneer life.
• Well spoken	• Test on facts about westward expansion, life on the prairie, and basic geography.
	• Explanation of memory box contents.
	• Quiz on facts about Native American tribes living on the plains.

Figure B.6

Social Studies Unit *(continued)*

Stage 3—Learning Plan
Summary of Key Learning Events and Instruction
The key to the transfer and meaning goals is that students need to be helped to process Prairie Day, the readings, and other events in terms of the essential questions. The aim is for students to say, in their own words, what prairie life was like and how pioneers then compare to pioneers now.
• Pre-assess: Use K-W-L to assess students' prior knowledge and identify further student-identified learning goals for the unit.
• Revise Prairie Day activities (e.g., substitute Oregon Trail 2 computer simulation for "dress the pioneer" and ask for prompted journal entries related to the EQs while the simulation is played). Students are helped to process the prairie day simulation, with the essential questions as the source of inquiry and talk. Students should see and be familiar with the questions and be encouraged to consider them on their own.
• Include other fictional readings linked to the identified content standards and understandings (e.g., *Little House on the Prairie, Butter in the Well*). Add nonfiction sources to accommodate various reading levels, such as *Life on the Oregon Trail, Diaries of Pioneer Women*, and *Dakota Dugout*. Guide students in researching the period, using a variety of resources. Link all readings back to the EQs.
• For acquisition as well as understanding, ask students to develop a timeline map of a pioneer family's journey west.
• To prepare students for transfer, have them develop ideas about how we are all pioneers in some ways, and research current pioneers.
• Stage a simulated meeting of a council of elders of a Native American tribe living on the plains to have students consider a different perspective and develop empathy for the displaced Native Americans. Discuss: "What should we do when threatened with relocation: fight, flee, or agree to move (to a reservation)? What impact would each course of action have on our lives?"
• Teacher supplies graphic organizers and prompts to help students reflect upon the readings and learning events concerning the nature of a pioneer and the effects of cultural interactions between pioneers and native peoples.
• Review the scoring rubrics for memory box, museum display, letters, and journals before students begin the performance tasks. Include opportunities for students to study examples of these products.

Source: Goals © 2000 California Department of Education. All rights reserved.

Source: © 2004 ASCD. All rights reserved.

Examples of units from different grade levels and subjects and topics are available online. Figure B.7 shows an Algebra Unit Before UbD; Figure B.8 shows the Algebra Unit after applying UbD. Additional sample units are also available: Figure B.9 Music Unit, Figure B.10 Literature Unit, Figure B.11 Climate Unit, Figure B.12 Visual Arts Unit, Figure B.13 Health and PE Unit, Figure B.14 History Unit, and Figure B.15 Time Unit.

Further Information on the Ideas and Issues in This Module

Understanding by Design, 2nd ed. (Wiggins & McTighe, 2005). Chapter 1 discusses the backward-design approach to unit design. Chapter 11 describes the original UbD Template and presents a "before" and "after" UbD unit for geometry.

Schooling by Design: Mission, Action, and Achievement (Wiggins & McTighe, 2007). Chapter 1 discusses the mission of education and shows how state standards at the highest level focus on transfer as a goal. Chapter 2 discusses the long-term goals of a curriculum as understanding and transfer, and Chapter 3 describes how such a curriculum could be developed.

References

Wiggins, G., & McTighe, J. (2005). *Understanding by design.* (2nd ed.). Alexandria, VA: ASCD.
Wiggins, G., & McTighe, J. (2007). *Schooling by design: Mission, action, and achievement.* Alexandria, VA: ASCD.

Module C

Starting Points

Purpose: To consider appropriate starting points and sequences for unit design, given your style, interests, and needs.

Desired Results: Unit designers will understand that

- Neither *The Understanding by Design Guide to Creating High-Quality Units* nor the UbD Template requires a lock-step approach to design. Although the template has a logical layout for the design *product,* it does not demand a single step-by-step design *process.*

Unit designers will be able to

- More effectively decide where and how to begin and work through their specific unit design, based on their style, interests, and unit topic.

You should work on Module C if you are unsure of the scope and direction of your unit, and if you want ideas and advice on where to begin and how to proceed.

You might skim or skip Module C if you are familiar with backward design or very comfortable with your own approach as a unit designer. In that case, you might want to go to Module D to sketch a unit or to Module E to begin to develop a unit in the full template. If you are comfortable with your skills and approach as a designer but are not sure exactly how best to develop a unit devoted to understanding, you might skip ahead to the "Design Decisions" section of this module, beginning with Question 3 about unit scope.

Like students, educators differ. We vary by the subjects and grades we teach, our prior experiences with curriculum planning, design methods, interests, and needs. Accordingly, the *Guide to Creating High-Quality Units* has been organized to be as flexible as possible.

The module structure also accommodates varied design and learning styles. You may prefer to go step-by-step, or you may be one of those designers who works holistically and in a nonlinear fashion; the modules are written and organized to permit this, particularly if you refer back to the chart of modules in the introduction for guidance (see Figure 1). You may be happy with a blend: following each module step by step for a while, but then going back to earlier modules as the demands of later work on your unit suggest the need to do so. The stand-alone nature of the modules permits this, too.

As you may have already noted, we begin each module with suggestions as to whether this one might be right for you at this phase of your work or whether it would be more fruitful to move to another one. In short, you can proceed sequentially, iteratively, or skip around in the guide. As long as you remain always aware of the ultimate product—a well-designed and aligned unit in the UbD Template—your preferred approach should work with what we provide.

Product Versus Process

However you are most comfortable working as a designer, beware of a common misconception: that the look and logic of the *Guide to Creating High-Quality Units* and the UbD Template provide a directive about the chronology and process of design. This is not the case. The *Guide* reflects the look of the template, and the template provides a vehicle for the final product of your design work. The creative process is always more messy and back-and-forth across design elements than the final product.

A simple analogy for the relationship between process and product with the UbD Template is the printed recipe in any cookbook. Readers can see and follow the recipe easily because the cook has made sure to clarify the chronology of the work to be done. But this logical approach to offering a recipe as the product of work almost always hides the messy, back-and-forth process by which the recipe was developed, tested, refined, and completed. To put it bluntly, the cook did not follow the recipe to create the recipe! There can never be a recipe for creative and effective design, whether in creating a meal, a building, or a curricular unit. Rather, the recipe or blueprint—like a polished unit in the UbD Template—reflects the final product in an easy-to-read and -use form.

Closer to academic work, think of the pagination of a final printed version of a text versus the chronology of the writing process by which the book took shape. It is extremely unlikely that the author wrote the first pages in the finished book first. In fact, the introductory pages were probably written very late in the process, as the book was developed. The same is true in unit design. It may be fairly late in the process that we articulate to ourselves the point of the unit, the *key* understanding we are after. Then, of course, the unit has to be edited to account for that insight.

Design Decisions

Mindful of differences in reader styles, we nonetheless can identify a few fruitful design pathways, based on our experience working with thousands of educators from all grade levels and subjects. Our recommendations will be more useful if you undertake a brief self-assessment of your style, interests, needs, and aspirations by considering the following nine questions.

   1. What kind of a designer are you? Do you prefer a step-by-step approach to planning or do you first like to think about the whole and sketch out some ideas that you keep refining in a back-and-forth way over time? If you are the latter, you will more likely want to start with Module D, in which you make some rough sketches for a unit, worrying only broadly about the three stages of design instead of all the particulars of the template. If, however, you like to work step by step toward a complete, full UbD Template, you may want to skip Module D and go straight to Module E, in which Stage 1 is considered in greater detail.

   2. What kind of content goals will you focus on? What you teach may affect how you design. For example, teachers in subjects that focus heavily on skill development (e.g., literacy, foreign language, mathematics, physical education, careers and technology, music and art) often find it more comfortable to begin by considering transfer goals in some detail before getting too involved in tackling essential questions and understandings. Conversely, some designers whose teaching is typically focused on ideas and content knowledge (e.g., history/social studies, themes in literature, concepts in science or art) often prefer to concentrate initially on essential questions and their implications.

   3. What is the scope of your unit? You know that the goal in UbD is student understanding, so it would probably be unwise to focus your unit on a few minor facts or simple subskills out of context. Presumably, the best units for aiming at student understanding involve inquiries, challenges, issues, themes, or problems that require learners to make sense of something of sufficient scope and substance to permit in-depth exploration. Such exploration would entail a unit focus on key principles, core processes, an important text, or the strategic applications of various skills to meaningful issues, problems, or performances. In other words, the best units do not focus on a fact or a skill; they focus on how to use related facts or skills to achieve understanding. The ideas in Figure C.1 may be of help, therefore, in picking a worthwhile entry point.

   4. Is it best to start with a new unit or revise an old unit? Sometimes the best way to learn a new approach is to start fresh, with the proverbial blank piece of paper. At other times, beginners to UbD find it easier to start with an existing unit that they know well and reframe it through the lens of UbD. Either approach can work. (Of course, work from a unit that isn't your best. You then have some incentive to improve it via UbD!)

Figure C.1

Starting Points in Unit Design

Where to Start	Where *Not* to Start
A "big" state/provincial standard that encompasses content knowledge, skill, and higher-order thinking and application (e.g., "creative writing" or "regrouping and factoring to solve problems")	A "narrow" standard, benchmark, or indicator that focuses on a discrete skill or content objective (e.g., "sonnets" or "the associative property")
Important, enduring ideas that are worth understanding (e.g., "Models enable us to test possible outcomes or effects")	A favorite learning activity (e.g., making a model volcano with baking soda and vinegar)
Topics with essential questions that must be continually revisited (e.g., Whose "history" is this? How precise do I have to be? How does culture shape art and vice versa?)	Questions with factual answers (e.g., What is the chemical symbol for iron? What is alliteration? How do you add fractions?)
Performance weaknesses revealed by assessments (e.g., students have difficulty making inferences about the main idea or solving multistep/nonroutine math problems)	Basic knowledge or skill deficits revealed by assessments (e.g., vocabulary, subtraction of two-digit numbers that involves borrowing)
Enduring ideas that are worth understanding—a universal theme, theory, or interpretive schema (e.g., "power corrupts")	Key facts, definitions, or a short reading
A powerful process/strategy for using many important skills (e.g., conducting a scientific inquiry)	A single important process (e.g., using a microscope)
An inquiry into complex issues or problems (e.g., WebQuest on sustainable energy options)	A basic skill that requires only drill and practice (e.g., keyboarding)

Because unit design is challenging work, it is also wise to think about your own interests and motivation. Do you feel enthusiastic about the idea of imagining a new unit in which you play with the ideas of UbD? Or do you want to address a more practical need related to some area of weakness—in either your own designs or student performance? Are you eager to explore UbD by developing a model unit? Or is your goal to use whichever UbD tools and techniques might help you improve an existing situation? If you are happy doing some out-of-the-box thinking when given the chance to, go for it! If you are more practical or pressed by circumstance to improve a very particular "reality," work there. Again, it only matters that the choice is deliberate and offers great opportunity. Either entry point is fine, but you should be resolved in your choice.

5. *What areas of need might be addressed?* Often the results of standardized tests or district/classroom assessments reveal important problems in student performance; this information offers useful entry points. Are there long-standing weaknesses in student achievement related to key goals that sorely need tackling? This may be an ideal time to address them. What is currently being done isn't working! Why not try some fresh thinking about a persistent deficit in student

performance? For example, many educators want to improve the critical thinking of students—and for good reason: test results and classroom observations show that many students (even many who are successful) are uncritical in their work. Therefore, why not start with a unit in which you deliberately target critical thinking using core content (or some other higher-order process) with which students typically struggle, such as summarizing a text, developing a sound thesis or hypothesis, or solving nonroutine problems? Figure C.2 offers some common "problem statements" we have encountered over the years. Perhaps one of them will provide you with a clearer direction for your design work.

6. *Do I have to start with a unit?* Perhaps this discussion of a unit-design entry point has left you feeling a bit uneasy, no matter how fruitful some of the entry points appear. "Shouldn't I first clarify the curriculum for the program and my goals for the course or year before embarking on a particular unit? Wouldn't that be the most logical thing to do?"

Our answer may strike you initially as odd, but it relates back to what we said earlier about logical product versus logical process. Theoretically, you are, of course, correct. Units must logically derive from pre-existing course syllabi or goals for the year, and from curricular frameworks that map the year in relation to our ultimate goals for the students' education. But we have found that for beginners in UbD, starting at such a level of generality and abstraction, although logical, is not very helpful for understanding and improving unit design. You are likely to be less overwhelmed and more effective working on one or two units before tackling the larger and more difficult task of UbD syllabus design or K–12 curriculum mapping. For a lengthier discussion of these "macro" curriculum issues, see Chapters 2 and 3 of *Schooling by Design* (Wiggins & McTighe, 2007) and Chapter 12 of *Understanding by Design* (Wiggins & McTighe, 2005).

As long as you can easily justify your initial unit focus in terms of existing program goals, state standards, or school mission, you can be confident that starting with unit design will serve you well. For those who insist on thinking first about the entire curriculum framework, we strongly recommend that you read the first three chapters of *Schooling by Design* (Wiggins & McTighe, 2007) and consult the related materials in *Schooling by Design: An ASCD Action Tool* (Zmuda, McTighe, Wiggins, & Brown, 2007) that map out the "macro" curriculum approach backward from mission and long-term program goals.

7. *What about beginning with a lesson?* Perhaps your uneasiness goes in the other direction, if your experience is primarily in designing daily lessons. What, then, does unit planning offer beyond traditional lesson planning?

As you might expect, the value of the unit over the lesson is the flip side of what we just said about units versus courses and programs. Far too many lessons are narrow, focusing on isolated and discrete objectives that do not coherently build toward an enduring understanding or independent performance ability. The result is often fragmented teaching and short-term learning. The "unit" by

Figure C.2

Common Problem Statements

Identify a statement, below, with which you agree. Based on your decision, frame your unit goals accordingly. Alternatively, add your own statement, or modify any sentence to suit you.

What You Often Observe in Student Performance and Behavior

1. Student performance on assessments is frustratingly weak, especially on questions/tasks that require in-depth understanding and transfer ability.

2. My students seem to have no sense of what really matters in my class; they seem to be unclear about year-long priorities and their primary responsibilities.

3. My students are very passive and reactive in their work. They have great difficulty solving their own problems, asking questions, thinking critically.

4. My students don't understand that understanding is my goal. They think all they need to do is give the "right" answer (or find it somewhere), they think learning is just recall, and they think that my job is to spoon-feed them—and they resist when I try to get them to justify answers or dig deeper.

Other:

What You Acknowledge Might Be True About Design Weaknesses

5. We tend to "cover" the content more superficially than we should (even though the classes might involve interesting discussions and experiences).

6. Our lessons have many "activities," but they often lack an overarching learning goal that is clear to learners. Lessons are sometimes just a lot of different and isolated experiences.

7. We ask students to do too many "drills" and not enough "playing the game" in our assessments. We have too few higher-order performance tasks in our assessments; our tests focus mainly on the first two levels of Bloom's taxonomy: recall, recognition, and plugging in of previous learning.

Other:

definition should embody a meaningful and connected chunk of learning events that build toward some important intellectual outcome in a way that short (often disconnected) daily lessons cannot. Arguably the most basic implication of an education for understanding is that it goes deeper, beyond the surface. It is not simply scattershot coverage of bits of content. Depth means that we look analytically and from different points of view at the same content; by necessity, that process takes place over many lessons.

Whether the unit is focused on a complex text (e.g., *Sarah Plain and Tall* or *The Great Gatsby*), an idea (e.g., "the water cycle" or the notion of a democracy based on "inalienable rights"), or a complex and worthy task (e.g., an elaborate role-play in Spanish, a scientific inquiry into laws of motion, or research on and presentation of a historical event), the lessons have to hang together and build toward complex performances and products. Instructional coherence requires thinking about a full unit of study made up of distinct but related and reinforcing lessons.

As we said earlier, it matters less where you begin than where you end up. So there is no need to fret too much about a starting point. *Just do it*, as the commercial says. Feel free to start where you are comfortable or curious—while mindful of the alignment needed across all three stages.

8. What's the role of my textbook in UbD unit design? The default approach to unit planning for many teachers is to use what the textbooks provide. This approach is unwise—no matter the quality of the textbook. Why? Because no textbook unit was designed backward from your goals, your local curriculum, your school mission statement, and your district or organization's K–12 goals. Like a very generic cookbook for diners of all sizes, tastes, and medical conditions, and cooks of varied skill, the textbook only provides generic possibilities that have to be shaped to suit your context and the "appetites" of your young charges. Consider the following characteristics:

- *Textbooks are typically organized by topic, not transfer goals.* Most textbooks are more like encyclopedias and computer manuals: they provide a thorough and logical set of content and discrete activities organized by topic. History is organized chronologically; geometry is organized by the movement from definitions and axioms to theorems. It does not follow that all this content, with its organization neatly laid out this way, directly addresses your goals or offers the best way to achieve them.
- *Textbooks generally place too much emphasis on acquisition of knowledge and skill and too little on meaning-making and transfer.* This characteristic is clearly reflected in the typical assessments provided (which tend to focus primarily on recall items and decontextualized skill checks) and the typical activities provided (which tend to require minimal inquiry and deep thinking by learners). Even if you derive many of your direct instruction lessons from the textbook, you will still likely have to identify the transfer

and understanding goals separately and develop appropriate assessments and activities for them.

- *Textbooks are not necessarily tailored to the variety of learning styles, interests, and ability levels in your classroom.* Although many textbooks provide ideas and materials for differentiation, this advice is inherently generic. It cannot fully respond to your particular classroom profile.

The bottom line is that a textbook should serve as a targeted resource, not a syllabus. Accordingly, you have to design a unit that addresses *your* desired results for *your* students, and reference only the relevant elements of the textbook.

9. What might be a preferred entry point for me, mindful of the template? As we said at the outset, regardless of the layout of the UbD Template, you may find it most comfortable and useful to start with elements that play to your interests and background. Figure C.3 provides some prompting questions to help you in thinking through an entry point.

Various blank worksheets for getting started on unit design are available online (Figures C.4 through C.10), including a more detailed set of prompted worksheets for using each of the template entry points (content standards, important topic, important skill, key text, favorite activity, and key test).

Further Information on the Ideas and Issues in This Module

Understanding by Design, 2nd ed. (Wiggins & McTighe, 2005). Chapter 11 discusses the design process at length (note, however, that it refers to the earlier version of the template).

Understanding by Design: Professional Development Workbook (McTighe & Wiggins, 2004). Introductory worksheets and exercises are included.

References

McTighe, J., & Wiggins, G. (2004). *Understanding by design: Professional development workbook*. Alexandria, VA: ASCD.

Wiggins, G., & McTighe, J. (2005). *Understanding by design* (2nd ed.). Alexandria, VA: ASCD.

Wiggins, G., & McTighe, J. (2007). *Schooling by design: Mission, action, and achievement*. Alexandria, VA: ASCD.

Zmuda, A., McTighe, J., Wiggins, G., & Brown, J. (2007). *Schooling by design: An ASCD action tool*. Alexandria, VA: ASCD.

Figure C.3

Various Template Entry Points

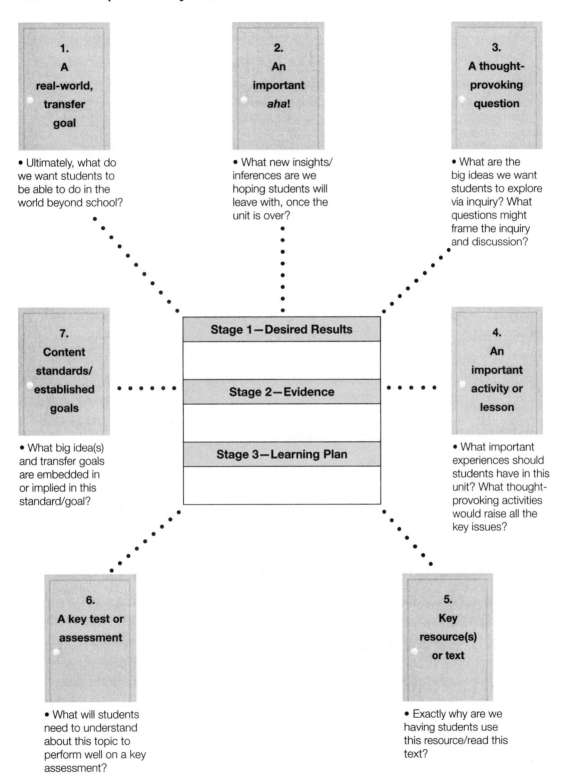

1.
A real-world, transfer goal

• Ultimately, what do we want students to be able to do in the world beyond school?

2.
An important *aha*!

• What new insights/ inferences are we hoping students will leave with, once the unit is over?

3.
A thought-provoking question

• What are the big ideas we want students to explore via inquiry? What questions might frame the inquiry and discussion?

7.
Content standards/ established goals

• What big idea(s) and transfer goals are embedded in or implied in this standard/goal?

Stage 1—Desired Results

Stage 2—Evidence

Stage 3—Learning Plan

4.
An important activity or lesson

• What important experiences should students have in this unit? What thought-provoking activities would raise all the key issues?

6.
A key test or assessment

• What will students need to understand about this topic to perform well on a key assessment?

5.
Key resource(s) or text

• Exactly why are we having students use this resource/read this text?

Module D

....

Developing an
Initial Unit Sketch

....

Purpose: To sketch an initial unit design using the three stages of backward design, with a focus on desired learning, not content coverage or teaching.

Desired Results: Unit designers will understand that

- Sketching a unit in all three stages enables designers to quickly experience the logic of backward design and its power.
- A backward-design template enables designers to efficiently check for unit alignment, which is key to all high-quality unit design.

Unit designers will be able to

- Sketch a new unit (or list the main elements of a previously developed unit) in the three stages of backward design.
- Check for unit alignment across all three stages.

The end product will be a unit sketch in the simple three-stage template.

You should work on Module D if you are unfamiliar with the backward-design process or new to Understanding by Design. You may also feel comfortable in starting your work with Module D if you are more of a holistic, draft-the-whole-unit-at-once type of designer (as opposed to a step-by-step designer).

You might skim or skip Module D if you are familiar with backward design and the UbD Template, or if you would prefer moving step-by-step through the entire template instead of sketching a whole unit and refining it. In that case, you might want to go to Module E.

....

We focus in this module on a quick unit sketch. Whether you work from a pre-viously developed unit or design a new one from scratch, the product goal is to develop a draft unit, briefly, using only the three stages of backward design (as opposed to the more detailed UbD Template described in Module B).

The basic logic of this design process is contained in three related questions (embodied in the three stages of unit design in UbD), as discussed in prior modules:

1. What are the desired long-term and short-term results of my unit?

2. What is appropriate evidence that learners have attained those desired results?

3. What are the most appropriate learning events for achieving those desired results?

Figure D.1 shows an example of an initial backward-design draft for a unit on nutrition. This unit will be improved based on UbD in subsequent modules.

Design Task: Using the nutrition unit example and our comments as a guide, sketch a new unit in the three stages (or list the main elements of a previously developed unit). You do not need to get too detailed. Simply list the main goals, assessments, and major learning events, based on the following questions:

- Stage 1: What should students learn as a result of this unit (short term and long term)?
- Stage 2: What assessment evidence will show that students have met the Stage 1 goals?
- Stage 3: What key learning events will help students reach the goals and be successful on the assessments?

Now that you have a beginning in the form of your design-task sketch, we will explore each of the three stages of backward design in a bit more detail. However, if you are completely comfortable with what you have sketched out so far and you understand the basic logic of the three stages, you might want to go to one of the other modules now. Otherwise, continue with this module to explore each stage in more detail.

Stage 1—What Are the Desired Results?

There is an old saying that "if you don't know where you are going, then any road will get you there." That statement expresses the opposite of designing backward from your destination. As we have said thus far, the destination must be framed in terms of changes in the student—the learnings sought (i.e., the student output)—not in terms of the content and your actions (i.e., the teacher inputs). The key to effective educational design is to think backward from the desired results of successful instruction, which is the student's ability to make use of what was learned. Then you'll more likely know the instructional path to get there (and avoid mere coverage, or merely pleasant activities).

Figure D.1

Simple Stages for Nutrition Unit

Unit Topic: Nutrition **Subject(s):** Health/PE **Grade(s):** 5 **Time Frame:** 4 weeks

Stage 1—Desired Results
This unit introduces basic concepts of nutrition. Students will learn about various types of foods and their nutritional values, the USDA Food Pyramid guidelines for a "balanced" diet, and various health problems that can result from poor nutrition. They will also learn how to read food labels for nutritional information.

Stage 2—Evidence
Students will be assessed through quizzes and a final test to assess their knowledge of nutrition, specific nutrition vocabulary, the food groups, and the Food Pyramid guidelines.

Stage 3—Learning Plan
Major learning activities include the following: • Learn and memorize nutrition vocabulary. • Read "Nutrition" chapter from the health textbook. • Learn about the USDA Food Pyramid and the food groups. • Watch video "Nutrition and You." • Create a class cookbook. • Listen to a guest speaker (nutritionist). • Learn to read food labels for nutrition information. • Plan healthy menu for class party. • Take final unit test.

So, you can't simply say, "I want my students to learn fractions" or "I want them to understand *Romeo and Juliet*." Those statements just restate the content that will be taught, not what students should have specifically learned from the encounter and be able to do with the content in the future. Nothing in those two "I want" statements says what we need to see in student performance as a result of the unit.

The following imaginary conversation between two teachers should sharpen this key idea of designing backward from "learnings," not mere "teachings":

What's your unit about?

It's about the Constitution and the three branches of government.

What are the desired results of the unit?

I want students to understand the Constitution and the three branches of government.

No, you just repeated the topic. What are the desired learnings about the topic?

Understanding the three branches of government and their different functions.

I am not being clear enough, I guess. That's the same answer—the topic. Having studied the Constitution and learned about the three branches of government, what will students come away having understood and able to do in the future?

I am unclear on your question. They should at least know all the key facts about what the Constitution says.

But is that really your only goal? What's the point, your reason for teaching these facts? What should they leave having grasped about those key facts? What should they now be able to see and do in their lives using such facts?

Hmm, I guess I am not sure what to answer when you put it that way. You don't want me to just list more specific "content" about the three branches, do you?

No. I am asking a question about the effect of your teaching. If they really did understand this content, what would they then see and do differently? What's the point of teaching that content?

Oh, *now* I see what you want. OK, how about this: I want students to understand that our government is organized so that no single group will have too much power, because there is a tendency for power to corrupt.

Great. Why does that understanding matter?

Well, as a result, there is a constant push and pull, where the branches constantly spar over restricted power. I want them to recognize that the way the government was set up long ago matters to us today—every day. For example, I want them to understand why there are congressional actions based on Supreme Court decisions, or why a president might veto proposed legislation, or why the two major parties disagree about how those powers are used.

Ah, now that's a clear understanding-focused goal! That's what I was asking for. That's what you have to design backward from—the understanding sought, not just the facts.

Do you see the difference? You want to design backward from these particular meaningful "take-aways," not simply from a list of content objectives. In other words, it's not true that the goal of a course of study is merely to "learn the content." The content is actually the means to some important intellectual end—new insight and ability in the learner in which content is meaningful and useful going forward.

Thinking backward from the changes in the learner's thinking and action takes some getting used to. We are so accustomed to thinking about just the short-term goal of content to be learned and activities for doing so that we have difficulty sometimes considering a few simple questions: Why are we teaching it in the first place? What are the long-term and bottom-line outcomes from the teaching that justify teaching it in the first place? What should the learner have accomplished, and be able to accomplish in the future, as a result of the activity and the content?

The stems below can help you more easily frame your content-related goals in terms of understanding and transfer:

- If that's the *knowledge*, what do you want students to understand about it?
- If that's the *skill*, what understanding(s) will enable students to more wisely apply it?

Thinking in this way requires you to do more than identify and teach worthy content. A central premise of UbD is that mastering a list of content objectives is not really the long-term desired result of *any* unit (though it may be the objective of a few lessons in the unit). If you want students to master a skill or two, why? If you want them to learn some words, dates, or other facts, why? In other words, what worthy long-term and real-world ideas and accomplishments does learning that particular skill or knowledge help you achieve? It's those longer-term and complex ideas and accomplishments requiring content knowledge and skill that are the bottom-line aims of teaching.

Skill-Focused Desired Results

Here is another conversation, this time about skill-related goals:

So, what's your unit about?

It's on graphing data.

What's the desired result of learning this skill? What's the point?

That they can graph data.

No, that's a skill. What's the point, the goal for having them learn such skill?

What do you mean?

If the unit is focused on a skill, what is the purpose of such a skill? Why learn it? What does that skill—and others related to it—enable you to do on your own that really matters? What transfer tasks require such skill?

Oh, I see. My goal is to help learners see how different visual displays can help people understand potentially confusing numbers and see patterns that may not be obvious. I also want them to understand that certain types of displays work better for some types of data and purposes. I want students to not only be able to interpret data displays, but also become skilled at creating appropriate displays for different situations.

Again, note the thinking inherent in a backward-design approach: by clarifying important understandings and abilities about visual display, the teacher can better plan to teach and assess them. What may not yet be fully clear but is very important is that the new answers about purpose will significantly affect how the content is assessed and taught in Stages 2 and 3, respectively.

How Long-Term Understanding Goals Shape Short-Term Teaching and Assessing of Content Acquisition

Long-term understanding goals will influence how you handle the short-term knowledge and skill acquisition goals. The most obvious implication is that because rote recall is not the long-term goal, merely teaching and testing for short-term recall is not an adequate instructional plan for achieving understanding.

Let's consider driver's education (the example used in Module B to help you better understand the template and UbD) to see how short-term work on skill and knowledge is always significantly shaped by an awareness of the longer-term meaning and transfer goals that justify teaching it. A driver's ed course must be designed backward from the student's ability to drive competently on real roads, not backward from a list of discrete skill and knowledge objectives that the teacher will "cover" and the learner will "do" in isolation. The real-world performance goal shapes not only the use of (very limited!) learning time but the methods of learning. If the goal were merely to pass a written test to get a license, then teacher talk, book reading, and quizzing only might make sense. But the task is to turn the novice into an adequate self-disciplined and thoughtful driver—a *user* of knowledge, skill, and understanding in real performance—in whatever small amount of time is available.

Mindful of the driver's ed analogy, then, think about transfer-type goals related to the core content of your unit—even if your habit has been to think of "content" as related to discrete ideas and knowledge.[1] What's the equivalent of "being able to drive successfully"—to effectively use the key knowledge and skill with understanding—for your unit? The following two prompting questions may be helpful in further clarifying the larger purposes of teaching skills:

- If that's the skill, what understanding will enable effective use of it and other related skills?
- If that's the skill, what tasks/situations will require effective use of this and related skills?

The Question of Purpose

We can reframe the challenge of clarifying our desired results by asking a different question—a question often on the minds of learners: What is the purpose of the teaching? In the end, what will this learning enable me to do or achieve that matters?

Any number of questions can be useful in clarifying the purpose of a unit:

- What's the point of the unit? "So what?"
- Why is this a unit worth teaching? Why does this content matter?

- What about this topic is most important? Most interesting?
- What about this subject captures your attention? Students' attention?

Or, consider these common student queries:

- Why are we learning this?
- Who in the real world ever uses this content to do work that matters?
- In the end, what will this enable us to accomplish in the world?

Students deserve an answer to such questions. Knowing where the learning is headed enhances focus and engagement. More to the point of good design, answering such questions as a teacher will help you avoid aimless coverage of content. So it is often useful for designers to answer the age-old student query about purpose in identifying goals in Stage 1. And as you may already have grasped, often the answer to such questions is a transfer or understanding goal.

When considering the bottom line, you are asking, "In the end, what should a learner eventually be able to *do* with this and similar content that really matters?" The point of school is not merely to be taught stuff or to get good at school. The point of education is to be able to learn in such a way that the learner (1) grasps the significance of what is learned and (2) can apply the learning wisely in the future—in other coursework and in life beyond the classroom.

Don't yet worry about the details of the unit. Just think about the unit's objectives in terms of eventual desired student capability. Try especially to resist thinking about basing the unit on only familiar activities and lessons (unless listing them helps you think of the bigger picture and purpose).

Stage 2—What Is Evidence of Achieving Unit Goals?

Stage 2 of backward design asks unit designers to "think like assessors" in light of such desired accomplishments. Suppose your goals were met. What specifically would you see that is convincing you that successful learning occurred? What would count as concrete evidence of achieving your desired results? What specific assessment tasks would best reveal if your broader goals had been achieved? These are roughly different versions of the same question, and they get at the issue of validity of assessment—that is, ensuring that the Stage 2 assessments align with the Stage 1 goals. (We consider validity in greater depth in Module G.)

In thinking about assessing your various goals, you are likely to be most comfortable with assessment of knowledge and skill, because these are measured with familiar methods. For example, if we want to see if students know multiplication tables or chemical symbols, then typical test items (e.g., items in a multiple-choice, matching, true-false, or fill-in-the-blank format) or direct questioning in class will provide appropriate evidence of accurate recall and simple "plugging in" in an efficient manner. Assessing for proficiency in a skill area (such as drawing a person from the side or adding sums correctly) requires only a simple demonstration of that skill. Basically, we look for accuracy when we assess for knowledge and skill; that is, did the student accurately recall the facts or correctly perform the skill, when prompted to do so?

Assessing for understanding is different and often more challenging than assessing for content acquisition. Where do we look, and what do we look for, to see if students genuinely understand what they also recall? How will we determine if they grasp subtle understandings or can make new meaning of the content? By what evidence can we convince ourselves that they understand well enough to transfer what they have learned (as opposed to merely plugging in knowledge and skill from memory)? In effect, the problem can be thought of in question form: What counts as evidence of genuine understanding? Students may know the right answer; does that mean they understand why it is the right answer and what it can be helpfully applied to?

In general, as we have already said, students show the extent of their understanding when they can (1) explain—in their own words—what inferences they have drawn and why (by providing appropriate evidence and reasons); and (2) apply their learning to new situations (i.e., transfer). Thus, at the very least, in Stage 2 we need to include assessment tasks that call for explanation and application. Students must not only give answers but justify them, and they should be able to apply their recent learning to new but related situations.

Understanding = Self-Prompting

Assessment of meaning and transfer involves an additional challenge. Earlier we asked, can the student correctly respond to knowledge or skill questions when prompted? But this is not what we mean by understanding, is it? We expect the student who has understanding to realize *which* facts and skills to use when—without having to be explicitly told just which facts and skills are wanted. In other words, understanding requires self-prompting and self-selection from one's repertoire of knowledge and skill. Whether confronted with a novel exam question or an unfamiliar-looking real-world demand (such as different road conditions when driving), we can only be said to truly understand if we recognize what is expected and act appropriately when the unnamed challenge presents itself. In the real world, there are no longer teachers or worksheets to scaffold, prompt, or remind us what to do. We would not say someone really understands a subject if he requires constant reminders and prompts about what specifically to do "here and now."

So assessing for understanding involves two demanding challenges: we must not only see if students can draw inferences and transfer them, but also see if they can do such explaining and applying with minimal reminders, hints, and prompting suggestions.

Design Tip: In your Stage 2 ideas, note that the bottom-line goal is for students to independently perform effectively with understanding, knowledge, and skill. You might find it helpful to explicitly use a version of that phrase in your early unit work to underscore that this is what the goal (Stage 1) really means and thus what the assessment (Stage 2) should call for. For example:

- **Stage 1:** Students should independently transfer their learning...
- **Stage 2:** The task requires students to independently recognize... (or apply... or explain...)

Assessment = Valid *Evidence*, Not Just Format

A common error when designing assessments is to decide on the format first and think that this decision is the only important one. "Let's see, you ask me what the assessment will be. Well, I'll have them do an essay on...." Hold on! The question being asked in Stage 2 is different and logically prior. *Regardless* of the format of the assessment, what are we looking for? What is evidence of understanding the content, no matter which format is used?

Whether the student does an essay, a speech, a project, or a diorama isn't the key issue in design. Rather, what will count as evidence of really grasping and applying the material and what will count as evidence of not understanding? Once we have thought through the evidence needs we are in a far better position to make a wise choice about assessment format and task particulars. Here's another conversation that illustrates what's at stake and the common confusion:

So what's your desired result?

I want students to understand linear relationships.

So what are you proposing for Stage 2?

Oh, we'll have a quiz on linear relationships.

No, that wasn't my question. What will you be looking for in the quiz? Regardless of whether you give a multiple-choice quiz or ask them to write using open-ended prompts, what counts as "understanding linear relationships"?

If they get my quiz questions right or wrong!

Well, of course. But which questions would best reveal understanding or lack of it? That is the assessment question. What must be built into the assessment, then, in order for you to get the evidence you need about their understanding?

Oh. Well, they have to be able to graph something like $y = 3x$.

Hold on. Couldn't someone know how to construct a graph like that from having just paid attention in class but without really understanding linear relationships?

I suppose so.

Well, then, go back to our basic definition: What should they "explain" or "apply" in order to show you that they really get that relationship?

Well, when you put it that way, maybe I am confusing my skill goal with my understanding goal. You could do that graph without really understanding why that must be the graph of the relationship and without grasping what that or any other such graph really means.

Yes. So what do you need them to show you if they are going to show an understanding of linear relationships in general?

They would probably need to explain why we call it a "linear" relationship, and that the essence of that relationship is that two things are in a constant ratio—that's why the graph has to be a line. They should also have to be able to explain the difference between a linear and a nonlinear relationship, and give me some tips for identifying whether some data is one or the other.

Yes! Do you see why that analysis is important for developing valid assessments?

I do. It makes me have to think carefully about just what my goal means and, thus, what the quiz should require of them; it's not just a question of skill in graphing or reading graphs, but can they say why it works and why it matters? That's what someone who understands can do.

Exactly. That's how you ensure validity of your assessments, if you design backward from the evidence you need, given the Stage 1 goals and what they imply.

Design Tip: Desired results and valid evidence of them are typically more general than the specific assessment tasks related to them. The goal of being an "accomplished speaker" suggests many possible tasks (e.g., a formal prepared speech, impromptu conversation, discussion) in many different situations (formal, informal, academic, social). The challenge is not to identify one specific task in Stage 2 but first to consider all the needed evidence against which we later build specific assessments for collection of that evidence. In other words, we would expect the same important goal to frame many units involving different assessment tasks and settings.

Consider an analogy to distinguish evidence versus task. If the goal is to be an "excellent athlete," then think of the decathlon as the evidence—results from a series of 10 specific and varied tasks that, if done well, signal achievement of the overall goal of excellence in athleticism.

Stage 3—Given the Goals and Evidence, How Might These Results Best Be Achieved?

Now it's time to complete a draft of your unit using Stage 3 of backward design. If you have determined the goals (Stage 1) and the evidence you will need to collect (Stage 2), what kinds of learning activities are most appropriate? What instruction is logically required? What is the best way to cause student learning, performance success, and goal accomplishment? Backward design is about logical alignment: *if… then…*. If that's the goal, then what follows for assessment and instruction?

If, for example, the goal is to make the student a more defensive driver when driving, and the assessments put students in situations where they show whether or not they drive defensively, then what follows for learning activities and instruction? How will they best gain knowledge, skill, and understanding about how to drive defensively on real roads under real conditions?

But recall our caution about understanding implying autonomy if the learning is to be effective. All learning plans for meaning and transfer need to be designed so that the learner is increasingly able to and expected to perform with independence. The instruction should involve decreasing reminders, hints, or other forms of scaffolding and prompting. In other words, if the learner is perpetually given reminders as to which content applies, what needs doing, and how to do it, then we should not be surprised by poor student performance on tasks requiring independent inference and application.

Similarly for critical thinking: if the goal is critical thinking and the assessments look for it, how will instruction develop and elicit it? This is an important issue in education. Many teachers fail to see that they aren't actively developing students' critical thinking; they merely hope it will occur. Worse, when lessons only emphasize recall, students do not need critical thinking for academic success; it falls through the cracks of conventional instruction and assessment.

The essential point here cannot be underscored enough, even if in the abstract the argument we are making is logical. Too often teachers identify learning activities and methods of instruction that are comfortable and familiar rather than thinking through which methods of instruction and approaches to learning will make it most likely that the unit goals are achieved. The following conversation reminds us of how easy it is to confuse familiar with appropriate instruction:

So what's your unit goal?

I want students to really understand how helpful it can be to think of our country in terms of regions.

OK. How are you going to assess their understanding? What evidence are you looking for of their understanding? In general, what are you assessing for?

I will ask them orally and in writing to explain both the advantages and disadvantages of the way we label and talk about the different regions of the United States.

What, then, are the key instructional moves?

Oh, it's all in our social studies textbook. The students will read about the Northeast, Southeast, Midwest, Southwest, West, and Northwest and describe the key characteristics of each region.

But isn't something missing? How will that help them critique the regional labels? How will just reading the text achieve the understanding you cited and show evidence of it?

Oh. I see the problem. Just because they might know about the various regions, if the book doesn't really get into the strengths and weaknesses of labeling the regions as we do, what then? Hmm. I'll need to organize some debates, perhaps, or help students do some research on how historians and geographers have actually changed their minds as to whether Missouri is in the Midwest or the South, for example.

The point here should be clear and constantly pondered: when we target important, long-term, higher-order goals (e.g., defensive driving, critical thinking), we must think carefully about what is required to help learners achieve them "by design," even if we feel pressed to focus primarily on acquisition of content or even if we are comfortable with our current teaching approaches.

Alignment in Backward Design: The Two-Question Test

As just mentioned, the logic of backward design suggests that the key elements of any unit design must align. What we put in Stage 3 must line up with (i.e., logically derive from) what we have listed in Stages 1 and 2; our Stage 2 assessment plan must logically derive from what our goals in Stage 1 demand. A simple way to act on this idea is to physically line up the elements in the three stages in your own draft template and draw connecting lines to ensure that the learning and the assessment ideas relate to all the goals.

Nor can this alignment check be done only once. A challenge once design is underway is to avoid saying, "OK, that stage is done—I'll move on. There's no need to return to that part," instead of always looking back to see how later work affects the earlier design. "Hmm. Now that I see all the lessons and learning activities, do I have all the right assessments?" Or "Given my goal of understanding, do I have enough of the right learning events?" To achieve alignment, designers are encouraged to use a circle-back approach instead of simply mentally checking off completed sections. Such ongoing self-assessment is an essential aspect of effective unit, course, and curriculum planning.

In concrete terms, any assessment or learning plan you design has to pass a pair of two-question tests at the heart of alignment in backward design. Here's the first set of questions:

- *Could students do the proposed assessment(s) well but not really have mastered or understood the content in question?*
- *Could students do poorly on the specific assessment(s) but really have mastery of the content in question?*

If the answer to either question is yes, then the assessment in Stage 2 most likely does not align with the understanding goal in Stage 1 that you initially linked it to.

Here's the second set of questions:

- *Could students do all the designer-proposed activities in Stage 3 but not really be ready to explain/justify/infer meaning or transfer their learning as demanded by assessments in Stage 2?*

> • *Could students fail to do all the proposed activities in Stage 3 but still be ready to handle tasks in Stage 2 that require higher-order inference and other kinds of meaning-making?*

If the answer to either question is yes, then the activities in Stage 3 most likely do not align with the goals in Stage 1 and the assessments in Stage 2.

Consider an actual example of an alignment/validity problem from a middle school social studies unit:

Stage 1 Goal—Students will understand the causes and effects of the Civil War, with an emphasis on political, economic, and military history. (This is a state standard.)

Stage 2 Proposed Assessment Task—Students will construct a diorama of a major battle of the Civil War and give an oral presentation on the battle.

Now we do the two-question test:

- Could students construct a great diorama and give an informative presentation but not really understand the causes and effects of the Civil War?
- Could students prepare a poor diorama or deliver a weak presentation but still really understand the causes and effects of the Civil War?

Clearly, the proposed assessment fails the test: yes is a likely answer for both questions. (In fact, a representation of a single event is rarely going to be the most helpful place to see evidence of understanding of cause and effect over time.)

Here's an example that points up the problem with typical quizzes:

Stage 1 Goal—Students will understand that fractions and decimals represent different expressions of the same quantities, and that efficiency, context, purpose, and audience determine which form to use when and why.

Stage 2 Proposed Assessment—A quiz involving the recall and plugging in of the algorithms learned for simplifying and converting fractions and decimals.

Now we do the two-question test:

- Could students do well on the quiz but not really understand that fractions and decimals represent different expressions of the same quantities or not understand when and how to use which form of mathematical expression in the real world?
- Could students do poorly on the quiz but still really understand when and why to use fractions or decimals?

Clearly, here too the proposed quiz fails the "test" of alignment (assuming that the quiz is the only assessment given). We would need more direct evidence of students' understanding of the equivalence and whether they can choose which form to use when and explain why. Try looking at your own proposed assessments of understanding in this light, and edit as needed.

The two-question test works with any proposed goal and assessment plan. Using this as a self-assessment is a good habit to develop, even when building simple quizzes. They, too, must provide valid results; that is, success or failure at the quiz should provide a strong logical link back to the goals it supposedly measures.

Stages 1, 2, and 3 need to fit together in the end. It doesn't matter precisely when or how often you double-check for alignment, but you have to be confident, based on a few careful analyses, that all stages ultimately connect. That's why the design standards and the template are designed the way they are—to remind us to do what we too easily overlook as we move on in our thinking. Odds are you will need to adjust your design multiple times, so the more you discipline yourself to self-assess the alignment a few times along the way, the better the final product will be.

We can summarize the work on crafting and self-assessing a unit sketch by saying that a key aspect of good design is to be clear about priorities and what meeting them looks like. Good teaching is not about marching through a long list of stuff and hoping that it all adds up to long-term fluent and coherent learning. Good teaching requires good planning, and good planning requires clarity about purposes and means of achieving them.

Self-Assessment—Review Criteria for Module D

Review your current unit sketch against the following self-assessment questions, and revise your design as needed:

- Are worthwhile, high-priority learning goals clearly stated in Stage 1?
- Do those goals provide a plausible rationale and motivation for teaching and learning the targeted content?
- Does Stage 2 contain valid assessment evidence of all the goals of Stage 1?
- Does Stage 3 sketch out the needed learning events and instruction, aligned with Stages 1 and 2?

Additional online resources for this module include the following worksheets with prompts to help you develop your initial unit sketch: Figure D.2, Simple Stages Template; Figure D.3, "If . . . , Then" Worksheet; and Figure D.4, What's the Point of My Unit?

Further Information on the Ideas and Issues in This Module

Understanding by Design, 2nd ed. (Wiggins & McTighe, 2005). Chapter 1 provides a detailed discussion of backward design, and Chapter 3 focuses on clarifying goals. Chapter 8 includes an extended discussion of the Civil War diorama example and the two-question test (see pp. 183–190).

Understanding by Design: Professional Development Workbook (McTighe & Wiggins, 2004). On pages 177–180 are a before-and-after version of the Civil War diorama example and a tool for the two-question validity test.

References

Bloom, B. (Ed.). (1956). *Taxonomy of educational objectives, handbook 1: Cognitive domain*. Chicago: University of Chicago Press.

Covey, S. R. (1989). *The seven habits of highly effective people: Restoring the character ethic*. New York: Simon and Schuster.

Gagné, R. (1977). *Conditions of learning* (3rd ed.). New York: Holt, Rinehart, and Winston.

McTighe, J., & Wiggins, G. (2004). *Understanding by design: Professional development workbook*. Alexandria, VA: ASCD.

Tyler, R. (1948). *Basic principles of curriculum and instruction*. Chicago: University of Chicago Press.

Wiggins, G., & McTighe, J. (2005). *Understanding by design* (2nd ed.). Alexandria, VA: ASCD.

---

[1]Some readers may think that we are arguing only for a simplistic "use" of knowledge and skill and thus suggesting that a liberal education or learning for deep understanding is not valued. Not so. If our goal as teachers is deep understanding of the subject, we will need to consider what that implies for specific outcomes. What is a liberal education meant to enable students to do and be like? What do historians, scientists, and mathematicians have to accomplish? In what sense is their discipline enabling them to be "disciplined" to behave in certain ways? Learning to "do" the subject might then be said to be the goal of rigorous academic courses.

Module E

Different Types of Learning Goals

Purpose: To distinguish the different types of unit learning goals (transfer, meaning, knowledge, skill) and draft a complete Stage 1.

Desired Results: Unit designers will understand that

- UbD distinguishes among four learning goals in unit design: transfer, meaning, knowledge, and skill.

- Each of the goals in UbD unit design has specific implications for assessment and instruction.

- The failure to acknowledge and address these different goals contributes to the problems of "coverage" teaching and the inability of learners to transfer their learning (a key factor in poor test results).

Unit designers will be able to

- Refine their unit sketch from Module D by distinguishing four types of goals (or develop four different goals for their unit if Module D was skipped).

- The end product will be a draft unit plan containing all of the Stage 1 elements: transfer (T), understandings (U), essential questions (Q), knowledge (K), and skill (S).

You should work on Module E if you are not sure how the goals of "understanding" (transfer and meaning) differ from conventional goals of "content acquisition" (knowledge and skill), and you have limited experience with essential questions.

You might skim or skip Module E if you are comfortable with the four goal types in the full UbD Template and their implications for assessment and instruction. If so, you may want to go to any later module.

One of the hallmarks of good unit design is the clarity with which inherently different, yet sometimes fuzzy, goals are specified and clarified. In this module, we concentrate on the four distinct (but in practice, often interrelated) educational goals upon which the full template is built—knowledge, skill, understanding, and transfer—and consider their implications for unit design beyond what was discussed in Module B, where the template was introduced. We also further discuss essential questions and their role in framing UbD units.

Stage 1—Desired Results

The terms *knowledge* and *skill* are familiar to readers. Essentially, knowledge refers to having command of facts, definitions, and basic concepts (declarative knowledge), and skill refers to the ability to perform some action or process competently (procedural knowledge). As the heading on the template reminds us, both of these goals are about acquisition. They differ from one another in obvious ways: you may know the facts about the difference between a drill and a hammer but not have skill or know-how in using either; on the other hand, you may know how to use a ball-peen hammer but forget the term when asked what type of hammer is called.

But what about understanding as a goal? What's the difference between knowing lots of things and really understanding? To what extent is understanding required to become truly skillful? What is the relationship between knowledge, skill, meaning-making, and transfer? These questions often puzzle us once we start to ponder the distinctions and interrelationships.

Let's remind ourselves of the various meanings of the terms *understand* or *understanding* that came out of the initial exercise in Module A upon which the template was built. The following two phrases (or their equivalent) come to mind for many designers when describing what understanding looks and sounds like:

Students who "really understand" can

- Draw useful inferences, make connections among facts, and explain their conclusions in their *own* words.
- Apply their learning; that is, transfer it to new situations with appropriate flexibility and fluency.

As you have seen, these two meanings are embodied in the full UbD Template in Stage 1, at the top. We distinguish inferences and connections—understandings—from the effective application of prior learning in new situations—transfer; both are distinguished from knowledge and skill. What makes these distinctions useful and not just semantic or cumbersome? The implications for learning and assessment.

Students who can make connections and arrive at important understandings, with minimal teacher hand-holding, are seeing for themselves how facts, data, and experiences are connected, extended, or otherwise related. As the upper levels of Bloom's Taxonomy suggest, people who understand can analyze, synthesize, and evaluate information and situations independently, not just recall prior teaching and plug it in. People who understand can take prior learning and use it effectively when confronted with new intellectual challenges and contexts where their knowledge, skill, and understanding are needed.

Consider again our driver's education example to further sharpen your understanding of the differences and relationships between the four goals. (You may want to look back at the example of Stage 1 for the unit on driver's education in Module B, Figure B.2, p. 18.) It is not enough to have mastered the discrete skills of braking and turning, or to know the rules of the road (the acquisition goals). Learners have to have developed a general understanding of what varied road conditions demand of them and internalized the idea of "defensive driving" (meaning); and they have to be able to apply their understanding, skill, and knowledge in varied, real-world road conditions—on their own (transfer).

Note, then, that although knowledge and skill are necessary for making connections and application, they are insufficient, by themselves, to cause the ultimate understanding or transfer needed for achieving the long-term goal of independent, safe, and savvy driving. Learners could know and do a lot of discrete things but still not be able to effectively see the big picture or effectively put it all together in context. Meaning-making and transfer are different achievements than acquisition, requiring different learning and teaching strategies (and, as we shall see, different assessments, too).

To illustrate the value of these distinctions (i.e., to help you with *your* meaning-making) and to help you better analyze your unit goals (i.e., to help you with *your* transfer task of unit design), let's consider these four goal types for various academic topics. Notice in Figure E.1 how we have categorized each of the goals as transfer (T), meaning (M), knowledge (K), and skill (S).

Design Task: Either review the draft unit goals you developed for Stage 1 in Module B and code each in terms of these four categories, or draft your unit goals for eventual placement in the full UbD Template.

- Which are the *knowledge* goals? Put a *K* after each one.
- Which are the discrete *skill* goals? Put an *S* after each one.
- Which are the *understanding* goals? Put an *M* after those that call for *meaning-making* via big ideas and a *T* after any involving *transfer.*

Note what we are doing in the module as an example of the very ideas being discussed. We first help you make better sense of the four terms (meaning). Now we are asking you to apply that meaning to your own design work (transfer).

Figure E.1

Examples of Four Goal Types

Topic: The American Revolution (Declaration of Independence)
• Know the names of the writers of the Declaration of Independence. **K**

• Use your research skill to learn about one of the signers of the Declaration. **S**

• Analyze the Declaration in terms of the historical context and its "audience" and "purpose" and develop a thesis about this document. **M**

• Apply your analysis to role-play a signer of the Declaration in a simulated town meeting where you explain your decision to your townspeople and are prepared to respond to criticism of your stance. **T**

Topic: Beginning Spanish
• Know the most common phrases related to asking directions. **K**

• Use your emerging skill with the present tense (and your knowledge of common phrases) to translate simple teacher prompts that begin *Donde está ...? * **S**

• A student argues "One past tense is enough, and it's too hard to learn two! Why bother?" Write a letter, make a podcast, or create a YouTube video on why different past tenses are needed for precise communication in Spanish. **M**

• Role-play: In a simulation of being in a crowded train station with little time, you must ask about various trains that have departed and will soon depart. Some speakers will speak more quickly and idiomatically than others. **T**

Topic: Linear relationships in algebra
• Know the meaning of "slope" and that $y = mx + b$. **K**

• Graph various linear pairs. **S**

• Explain, in general terms, how linear relationships help you find the price point but are not likely to help you predict sales. **M**

• Use linear equations and real data from experiments to help you determine the price point for selling store-bought donuts and homemade coffee at athletic events in order to make a profit for a fund-raiser. **T**

What Follows for Stages 2 and 3?

Once you have entered and coded your draft goals in Stage 1, it is a good time to practice some quick backward-design thinking with your draft unit: Given the four types of goals, what follows for assessment in Stage 2 and learning in Stage 3? For example, what do the goals you coded as "meaning" and "transfer" suggest for the needed assessment evidence? Will your usual approaches for assessment effectively reveal this understanding? Similarly in Stage 3: Were any proposed learning activities sketched in Module D or brainstormed just now sufficient to help students make meaning of important ideas? To transfer their learning? Although later modules address these questions in greater detail, you no doubt have some ideas now, and you should draft them out.

Really Understanding Versus Only *Seeming* to Understand

Perhaps you are still uncertain about how to transfer the idea of the four goal types into your unit sketch. The problem may be that you are still unsure about what we mean when we say we want students to "understand" content, not just "know" it.

In fact, it is surprisingly easy to conflate understanding with knowledge (as well as to confuse "transfer" with "scripted skill"). Just because we know a lot of important things and sound like we understand what we are talking about doesn't mean we do. Just because students seem skilled when we look at their performance doesn't mean they can transfer their learning. This nagging concern is key to making progress in UbD and as a teacher generally. The more we carefully analyze our educational goals and means, the more we realize that our obligations involve more complexity and uncertainty than we perhaps initially believed.

Let's remind ourselves that the word *understand* is really different in meaning from the word *know*. A genuine understanding that you really see and grasp for yourself is surely different from just being told and repeating someone else's claim (without necessarily getting the idea, what lies behind it, or how to use it). Just because you "know" that $A^2 + B^2 = C^2$ doesn't mean you understand it—that is, understand the "why" and the "so what" of it. Similarly, there is a difference between highly polished but completely scripted skill versus the ability to adapt your skills to new demands; the drill is quite different from the game.

Common sense and familiar language usage reveal the nuances. We say that understanding requires you to "explain in your own words" and "show your thinking." Why? Because your explanations provide evidence of your ability to have made sense of and use what you have learned.

Consider an example related to determining patterns. Suppose we ask you to find the pattern in the following series of numbers: 1, 1, 2, 3, 5, 8. Perhaps you do not see a pattern. Now, if we tell you that the pattern is "the next number in the sequence is the sum of the previous two," you don't necessarily understand the meaning of what we said. You just know we told you a rule. You could presumably restate what we just said if asked "So, what's the rule?"—without, however, really understanding what it is you are saying or what it implies for the next number.

It becomes a meaningful pattern that you understand and can apply only if you say, "Oh! I see it now: 2 + 3 = 5, and 3 + 5 = 8." Hearing you say this, in your own words, makes us realize you now probably understand. However, we would be more confident that you really get it if you could also extend your learning—for example, you could state the next several numbers in the series (13, 21) and explain how you determined them, and explain why the first two numbers are the same and why that is the only time that can happen (zero is implicit, and 0 + 1 = 1). You now clearly *see the bigger picture* on your own; you can *go beyond the information given* and *make sense* of what you learned. These are all roughly synonymous phrases.

Here is a knowledge-related example. If a student says that the Civil War was caused by moral disagreements about slavery, we might assume that she understands a cause of the Civil War. But we cannot be certain of this—yet. If the student wasn't helped to draw and to test these inferences or to see their logic from the facts (and reveal to us that she follows the logic and can confirm it), she can't yet be said to have made the connections, grasped the significance, or provided justification for it. What she may only have done (often without realizing it) is stated a claim that a teacher or text taught her. She may not be able to defend this claim in the face of counterclaims by other teachers or texts.

People with an understanding are not limited to "knowing" only what they were taught the way they were taught it; they can use their knowledge and skill to make connections, explore alternative perspectives, and adapt prior learning to new situations. That's why even a simple quiz that asks students to answer questions framed in a manner different from how they learned the content can stump some who seemed (to themselves, as well as you) to have "gotten" it the first time. Distinguishing between understanding and factual knowledge is arguably one of the biggest challenges in teaching, and failing to do so is an easy trap to fall into if you mostly "cover" content and quiz students to see if they have learned it. Students may seem to get it when they really don't, if the assessment really demands accurate recall only. However, they can be said to understand only if they can explain *why* in their own words, or extend that meaning or skill to achieve further understanding of related facts, data, stories, tasks, and events. In short, simply teaching accurate information can never ensure that students will understand. Their understanding has to be "tested" in the broadest sense of that term, just as an athlete is "tested" through competition versus mere drill. Figure E.2 elaborates the distinction between understandings and facts.

This distinction is true of skills as well as knowledge. Students may be able to divide 14.3 by 6.1, but if they cannot explain why it is permissible to move the decimal point (by multiplying each element by 10) to solve the problem, then they don't really grasp what they are doing—and that failure will play out in later work. In other words, if they cannot explain why 14.3 divided by 6.1 is equivalent to 143 divided by 61, then they don't really understand the underlying mathematical concept of equivalence and place value, why it works, and how it is used to solve problems. This lack of understanding of place value and how to simplify a new problem will hamper future attempts at mathematical problem solving. The examples in Figure E.3 should further clarify the difference between "getting it" and only seeming to "get it."

The essence of coming to an understanding, in other words, is that the students don't just follow someone else and repeat the other person's words; they draw inferences on their own. An understanding is not a fact; it is a conclusion based on facts (and one's own logical thinking).

Here is an age-old way of thinking about such understanding: Aesop's Fables. As you no doubt recall, the fables present a story of an animal or an insect (e.g., crow, fox, grasshopper, ant) confronting a situation. Each fable leads to a moral—a generalization that transcends the particular facts of the story. Here is an example:

The Ant and the Chrysalis

An Ant nimbly running about in the sunshine in search of food came across a Chrysalis that was very near its time of change. The Chrysalis

Figure E.2

Distinguishing Understandings from Factual Knowledge

Understandings	Factual Knowledge
• Reflect "big ideas" in the form of powerful generalizations. • Are transferrable across situations, places, and times. • Must be "earned" (i.e., constructed in the mind of the learner) through processes of inquiry, inferencing, and rethinking. • Are most appropriately assessed through performance tasks requiring one or more *facets of understanding* (e.g., application and explanation).	• Consists of *facts* (e.g., 4 x 4 = 16) and basic *concepts* (e.g., sky). • Facts do not transfer. Basic concepts have limited transfer capacity (e.g., the concept of *dog* applies to different breeds). • Can be learned in a rote fashion (i.e., without understanding). • Can be assessed using objective test/quiz items having a "right" or "wrong" answer.

Other Points to Remember

• An understanding is an inference, not a fact. It is a helpful insight derived from inquiry. Key understandings in intellectual fields (e.g., in physics: *Objects remain in motion at a constant velocity if no force acts on them*) often violate common sense and conventional wisdom. They are thus often prone to misunderstanding by students. Therefore, they cannot simply be "covered"; they must be "uncovered" (e.g., by exploring essential questions, wrestling with challenging problems, debating a complex issue).

• Such understandings endure in that they enable us to make vital and informative connections in our learning—as students and as adults. For example, the idea that "might does not make right" applies to both playground disputes and international diplomacy.

• Although facts and basic concepts can be learned in rote fashion, research shows that an understanding-based approach can yield more substantive, long-term, and flexible learning of the basics. Understandings function by helping to link and connect otherwise discrete facts and skills.

moved its tail and thus attracted the attention of the Ant, who then saw for the first time that it was alive. "Poor, pitiable animal!" cried the Ant disdainfully. "What a sad fate is yours! While I can run hither and thither, at my pleasure, and, if I wish, ascend the tallest tree, you lie imprisoned here in your shell, with power only to move a joint or two of your scaly tail." The Chrysalis heard all this but did not try to make any reply. A few days after, when the Ant passed that way again, nothing but the shell remained. Wondering what had become of its contents, he felt himself suddenly shaded and fanned by the gorgeous wings of a beautiful Butterfly. "Behold in me," said the Butterfly, "your much-pitied friend! Boast now of your powers to run and climb as long as you can get me to listen." So saying, the Butterfly rose in the air, and, borne along and aloft on the summer breeze, was soon lost to the sight of the Ant forever.

Moral: Appearances can be deceptive.

So when thinking of the "understandings" sought in Stage 1, think of the phrase *the moral of the story.* Analogously, if your unit is a story, what is the moral of your story? In other words, what general, useful, and interesting inferences do you want students to see as meaningful? That's what should go in the Understandings box.

Let's isolate some of the understandings from the sample units in Module B to see that although they may sound like "facts" that should go in the Knowledge box, they are really meant to be inferences that teachers will help students draw and grasp for themselves:

- Driver's Education—The time needed to stop or react is deceptively brief, thus requiring constant anticipation and attention. (See Figure B.2)
- Social Studies—Successful pioneers rely on courage, ingenuity, and collaboration to overcome hardships and challenges. (See Figure B. 6)
- Algebra—We can use the commutative, associative, and distributive properties to turn complex and unfamiliar expressions into simpler and familiar ones to solve problems. (See Figure B.8)
- Visual Arts—Artists use narrative conventions similar to oral and written storytelling to tell stories. (See Figure B.12)
- Health and Physical Education—A muscle that contracts through its full range of motion will generate greater force. (See Figure B.13)
- History—There are often different perspectives on what happened in the past; one's experiences influence one's view of history. (See Figure B.14)

Figure E.3

Successful Meaning-Making

Students show that they understand when they	Students have not yet made meaning if they
• See a pattern in the data (e.g., in the data, text, historical events) on their own. • Explain in their own words or own way (e.g., visual representation).	• Can only restate what they were told the pattern was. • Don't know how to look for a pattern or confirm for themselves that this is the pattern.
• State what the story means or provide a summary in their own words. • Realize that you have to read between the lines to make inferences about character, motives, feelings.	• Only read literally, and retell the plot, setting, characters, and so on. • Can only state facts from the story or repeat what others say the story means. • Are puzzled by inferences others make.
• Connect facts about people and events in a historical narrative to observations and generalizations they have made about such experiences. • Make generalizations about a historical period in their own words.	• Can only repeat a conclusion offered by the teacher or textbook, or only cite facts. • Do not make (or see the need to make) any connections to their own experiences or judgments about people and history. • Cannot accurately summarize or generalize about a historical period.
• Realize that the speaker of another language has made a joke or spoken sarcastically.	• Translate word-by-word and do not draw inferences about the speaker's intent.

Do you see what can be inferred from these examples? All these statements are generalizations: they must be *comprehended*, not just *apprehended*. They are not obvious or true by inspection or on faith. We are expected to see them as logical conclusions. Readers should infer, therefore, that to really understand what they mean requires that the learner infer them (or verify them, if they are first stated by others) from varied experiences—in the same way we just asked you to do here and in all the earlier exercises on the nature of understanding!

Transfer: What It Is and Isn't

Transfer goals highlight the effective uses of understanding, knowledge, and skill we seek in the long run—that is, what we want students to be able to do when they confront new challenges, both in and outside school, beyond the current lessons and unit.

Each subject area has a small number of overarching transfer goals. For example, a long-term aim in mathematics is for students to be able to solve any problem on their own. A long-term transfer goal in history is for students to apply the lessons of history to contemporary issues and to become more proactive citizens based on their understanding. In world languages we want learners to be able to communicate effectively in the target language, in different situations. In every case, the ability to transfer learning manifests itself in not just one setting but in varied real-world situations.

Furthermore, as suggested here, transfer is about *independent* performance in context. Students can only be said to have fully understood if they can apply their learning without someone telling them what to do and when to do it. In the real world, no teacher is there to direct and remind them about which lesson to plug in here or there. Transfer is about intelligently and effectively drawing from their repertoire, independently, to handle new contexts on their own. Thus young drivers must be able to handle all the varied and novel real-world situations that come their way. They must make constant judgments about the meaning of road conditions, and they must transfer their knowledge, skill, and understanding effectively, on their own. The goal of transfer thus requires that an instructional plan (in Stage 3) help the student to become increasingly autonomous, and the assessments (in Stage 2) have to determine the degree of students' autonomy, not just how much they understand the content. (A well-known approach to developing autonomy is called the "gradual release of responsibility" by the teacher, but we prefer to focus on the student's trajectory because that is the goal of education: student autonomy.)

Transfer goals have several distinguishing characteristics:

- They require *application* (not simply recognition or recall).
- The application occurs in *new situations* (not ones previously taught or encountered; that is, the task cannot be accomplished as a result of rote learning).

- The transfer requires a thoughtful assessment of which prior learning applies here; that is, some *strategic thinking* is required (not thoughtless plugging in of highlighted skills and facts).
- The learners must apply their learning *autonomously* (on their own, without coaching or teacher support).
- The learners must use *habits of mind* (e.g., good judgment, persistence, self-regulation) along with academic understanding, knowledge, and skill to persist with the task and polish the work to suit purpose and audience.

So what might be the transfer goals for your unit? Figure E.4 presents additional examples of transfer goals with explanations to help you better understand the concept.

Design Task: Given the discussion, examples, and exercises regarding understanding and transfer, review your understanding (transfer and meaning) goals for Stage 1. Revise or refine as needed.

Self-Assessment—Review Criteria for Module E

Review your current unit draft against the following self-assessment questions, and further revise your unit design as needed:

- Are all learning goals (including those derived from established standards) in Stage 1 properly coded as transfer (T), meaning (M), knowledge (K), and skill (S)?
- Do the identified goals in the Understandings box reflect important and useful "big ideas" or important applications of the learning?
- Do the stated goals in the Transfer box reflect genuine long-term accomplishment?
- Are the understanding goals framed by thought-provoking and open-ended essential questions?

The Nutrition Unit Revisited

We conclude this module by revisiting the nutrition unit introduced in Module D (see Figure D.1, p. 44). As shown in Figure E.5, the Stage 1 goals are now coded according to transfer, understanding, knowledge, and skill. The unit now also contains essential questions.

Online you'll find several worksheets to help you develop and clarify your goals: Figure E.6, Summarize the Relationships Among the Four Goal Types; Figure E.7, Coding Stage 1 Goals; Figure E.8, Implications for Stages 2 and 3 of the Four Goal Types; Figure E.9,

Sample Implications for Stages 2 and 3 of the Four Goal Types; Figure E.10, Clarifying Transfer Goals; Figure E.11, Considering Long-Term Transfer Goals, and Figure E.12, Clarifying Meaning Goals.

Figure E.4

Examples of Transfer Goals

Long-Term Transfer Goals	Why (and When) These Are Transfer Goals
Writing—Effectively write in various genres for various audiences, in order to • Explain (narrative). • Entertain (creative). • Persuade (persuasive). • Help perform a task (technical). • Challenge or change things (satirical).	The goal is to prepare students to use their writing repertoire for real-life demands with any combination of purpose, audience, and genre. The students transfer their prior learning when they write without explicit reminders and graphic organizers.
Mathematics—Recognize and solve never-before-seen mathematical problems in which it is not clear what exactly the problem is asking and what the appropriate approach for solving the problem is. These novel-looking problems involve either theoretical or real-world challenges.	Students have to judge what any problem is really asking, which mathematics might best apply, and the optimum solution path—all without being told how to proceed step-by-step. Transfer requires mathematical reasoning and strategy, not merely plugging in numbers in a familiar-looking exercise, via a memorized algorithm.
Health and Physical Education—Make healthful choices and decisions regarding diet, exercise, stress management, alcohol, drug use.	The long-term aim is to equip students with the knowledge, skills, and motivation to live a healthful life without nagging from parents and teachers.
Science—Evaluate scientific claims (e.g., X brand of paper towels absorbs the most liquid of all the leading brands), and analyze current issues involving science or technology (e.g., ethanol is the most cost-effective alternative fuel source).	Students understand scientific methods (e.g., need for validation) and habits of mind (e.g., healthy skepticism) to make informed decisions about science-related issues that they will encounter.
Reading—Read and respond to various types of text (literature, nonfiction, technical) through • Global understanding (the "gist"). • Interpretation (between the lines). • Critical stance. • Personal connections.	The goal is to prepare students to read and comprehend any text on their own.
History—Discuss the applicability of the history they have been learning to current and future events, and to other historical events and issues. What lessons, if any, should we learn from the past and apply to the present and other past events?	Students must consider the relevance of the past to the present, make judgments on their own, and apply them to specific issues.
Performing Arts—Create and perform an original work in a selected medium to express ideas and evoke mood/emotion.	The goal is to equip students for personal expression through the arts and to make aesthetic judgments about the arts on their own.
World Languages—Communicate effectively in the target language, in various situations with different challenges to understanding (speed, accent, over phone, etc.).	The goal is independent and successful communication in real-world situations where teacher prompts and reminders about the use of discrete knowledge and skills are not available.

Figure E.5

Nutrition Unit Outline for Stage 1

Unit Topic: Nutrition

Subject(s): Health

Grade(s): 5–7

Time Frame: 3 weeks

Stage 1—Desired Results

Transfer—Students will be able to . . .

• Evaluate their own eating patterns and make healthful nutritional choices.

Understandings—Students will understand that . . .

• Eating a balanced diet promotes physical and mental health, and enhances one's appearance and energy level.

• The USDA Food Pyramid defines healthy eating, but healthy eating varies for each individual depending upon age, lifestyle, culture, and available foods.

• Choosing healthy foods isn't always easy.

Essential Questions

• What should we eat?

• Are you a healthy eater, and how would you know?

Knowledge—Students will know . . .

• The food groups.

• The USDA Food Pyramid recommendations for a balanced diet.

• Key nutrition vocabulary (e.g., *protein*, *fat*, *calorie*, *carbohydrate*, *cholesterol*).

• Health problems caused by poor nutrition.

Skill—Students will be skilled at . . .

• Reading food labels for nutritional information.

• Planning a balanced meal.

Source: © 2004 ASCD. All rights reserved.

Further Information on the Ideas and Issues in This Module

Understanding by Design, 2nd ed. (Wiggins & McTighe, 2005). Chapter 2 is titled "Understanding Understanding," and Chapter 3 is about "Gaining Clarity on Our Goals." Chapter 5 covers essential questions, and Chapter 6 focuses on "Crafting Understandings."

Understanding by Design: Professional Development Workbook (McTighe & Wiggins, 2004). Pages 118–125 provide further exercises on distinguishing goals related to knowledge, skill, and understanding. Pages 88–118 offer exercises and worksheets on essential questions and understandings.

Schooling by Design: Mission, Action, and Achievement (Wiggins & McTighe, 2007). Chapters 1 and 2 discuss the educational goals of schooling and how to effectively write mission statements, program goals, and other long-term desired results.

References

Bransford, J., Brown, A., & Cocking, R. (Eds.). (2000). *How people learn: Brain, mind, experience, and school* (Expanded ed.). Washington, DC: National Academy Press.

Bruner, J. (1960). *The process of education.* Cambridge, MA: Harvard University Press.

McTighe, J., & Wiggins, G. (2004). *Understanding by design: Professional development workbook.* Alexandria, VA: ASCD.

Wiggins, G., & McTighe, J. (2005). *Understanding by design* (2nd ed.). Alexandria, VA: ASCD.

Wiggins, G., & McTighe, J. (2007). *Schooling by design: Mission, action, and achievement.* Alexandria, VA: ASCD.

Module F

Essential Questions and Understandings

Purpose: To specify the essential questions and understandings, based on the big ideas of the unit.

Desired Results: Unit designers will understand that

- Essential questions reflect the key inquiries and the understanding goals of the unit and thus serve to focus the unit and prioritize learning.

- An *understanding* is an inference that students are helped to draw or verify in the unit—even if the understanding sounds no different than a *fact*.

- In UbD, understandings are best framed as full-sentence generalizations, to specify the particular meanings we want students to make—and to avoid the common problem of thinking of a goal as just a restatement of the topic.

Unit designers will be able to

- Develop thought-provoking essential questions related to the unit topic and understanding goals.

- Precisely state the desired understandings as full-sentence generalizations.

You should work on Module F if you have not yet framed the unit understandings as full-sentence generalizations and have not yet generated companion essential questions, or if you think your draft understandings and essential questions need improvement.

You might skim and return later to Module F if you wish to explore the assessment implications of the different goal types in Module G or have already framed the unit understandings as full-sentence generalizations and have generated essential questions.

At the heart of teaching for understanding is the need to focus on unifying ideas and inquiries, not just discrete and disconnected content knowledge and skill. Big ideas reside at the core of expertise. They are embodied in a variety of forms, including the following:

- Unifying concepts (e.g., *the modern "flat" world of interdependence*)
- Organizing themes (e.g., *love conquers all*)
- Key strategies and rules of thumb (e.g., *turn complex quantities into the more familiar and simple to work with via mathematical equivalences*)
- Endless debates or issues (e.g., *nature versus nurture*)
- Striking paradox (e.g., *poverty amid plenty*)
- Dilemmas (e.g., *we simplify reality in math and science models—with some loss and possible oversight of important detail*)
- Persistent problems or challenges (e.g., *global warming*)
- Major theories (e.g., *Manifest Destiny*)
- Key assumptions (e.g., *markets are rational*)
- Key differing perspectives (e.g., *"terrorist" versus "freedom fighter"*)

Because big ideas are the basis of unified and effective understanding, they provide a way to set curriculum and instructional priorities.

For learners, big ideas make sense of lots of information and discrete skills. Without ideas to inform our perception and problem solving, every new situation would look unfamiliar, isolated, or puzzling. In other words, they are not *mere* ideas—that is, unhelpful abstractions. On the contrary, they illuminate experience; they are the linchpin of transfer, as Bruner (1960) noted long ago:

> The first object of any act of learning, over and beyond the pleasure it may give, is that it should serve us in the future.... In essence, it consists in learning initially not a skill but a general idea which can then be used as a basis for recognizing subsequent problems.... This type of transfer is at the heart of the educational process—the continual broadening and deepening of knowledge in terms of... ideas. (p. 17)

To show how big ideas inform understanding and transfer in all areas, consider these two examples where you might not expect them—team sports like soccer and basketball:

- *Create space on offense.* This big idea informs all offensive play. When the offense "creates space" (i.e., establishes larger areas of open field, court, or ice in which to work), the defense is spread out, making it more likely that a teammate will be "open" so that your team can receive and advance the ball and score. (The opposite is "bunching," which makes it much easier for the defense to defend the goal or stop advances.)

- *Legally deceive your opponent.* You can advance more successfully (and also create space more effectively) by "faking out" your opponents as to your ultimate direction or pace.

Notice that these two ideas are strategic in nature, not physical skills (like dribbling the ball or accurate corner kicks) or simple tactics (e.g., "use the give-and-go and the offsides trap—two ways to deceive your opponents and create space"). They are big ideas because they are general keys to success for using all your skills at any time. (Creating space in sports enables you to see more clearly and to find opportunities.) Moreover, strategic ideas are transferable to most team sports (e.g., football, ice or field hockey, water polo) and applicable at all levels of play.

Some ongoing inquiries, hence, essential questions, arise from these ideas:

- How can I create openings here, now? How can I and we as a team better avoid "bunching"?
- When and how should I deceive my opponents? Which moves work best, given my skill level and that of my opponents?

Let's look at a more academic example—writing—where teachers may tend to think that their job is only to teach skills, when, in fact, understanding and applying the skill appropriately are dependent upon ideas. The two big ideas at the heart of writing are now the familiar mantra of the writing process: audience and purpose. Expressed as questions, the organizing idea for all writers is always this: To whom am I writing? What is my purpose in writing? What effect do the answers have on what I say and how I say it?

So don't think of a big idea as a lifeless or vague abstraction. Think of it as a useful and illuminating conception or a focusing lens for helping students organize and make sense of their work and experience. In short, big ideas connect the dots of seemingly disconnected or disorderly content; they help turn data into information. Indeed, a major goal of UbD unit design is to identify the big ideas through which we can turn an enormous amount of content knowledge into interesting, connected, and useful inquiries (via essential questions) that culminate in specific and important meanings (understandings).

Design Task: Brainstorm big ideas for your unit. What one or two ideas can help the student make sense of all the content in the unit?

Big Ideas and the Template

You may be wondering: Where are big ideas placed in the UbD Template, since there is no designated box for them? Good question! Big ideas are actually reflected in several places, most obviously in the boxes for Essential Questions and Understandings. However, as we have noted, big ideas underlie successful transfer; thus they are also implied in the Transfer box.

Essential questions frame ongoing and important inquiries about a big idea, whereas understandings reflect important (but unobvious) answers—stated as full-sentence generalizations that we want our students to "come to" (in a meaningful way). Here's an example. The essential question "Why is that there?" sets up a lifelong inquiry into a big idea—the theory of "geography as destiny." As a result of exploring the question and the theory, we want students to come to specific understandings about that idea in different grade levels and courses. For example

- Human needs for food, work, commerce, and transportation often determine where people settle and cities grow.
- The geography, climate, and natural resources of a region influence how people live and work.

Notice that these understandings are not limited to a particular region or city. They are *transferable* across time and location in ways that facts are not. So the big idea of "geography as destiny" can be transferred to any new location, and that helps us better understand related cultural, historical, economic, and political experiences.

That idea of geography as destiny might then give rise to additional questions: Is a region defined primarily by geography? Or is it more related to culture? When ideas inform the study of content, it becomes far easier for students and teachers alike to generate interesting and helpful questions to frame learning—and to see that real learning requires and generates questioning.

Essential Questions

Thus, teaching for understanding demands that our designs and methods foster ongoing inquiry. A productive way to signal the importance of such inquiry is to base each unit on a few essential questions. Explicit and frequent reference to essential questions sends a powerful signal that a unit is about understanding, not merely the acquisition of knowledge and skill.

As suggested in earlier modules, we propose that a question is essential if it is meant to

1. Cause genuine and relevant inquiry into the big ideas of the core content.
2. Provoke deep thought, lively discussion, sustained inquiry, and new understanding as well as more questions.
3. Require students to consider alternatives, weigh evidence, support their ideas, and justify their answers.
4. Stimulate vital ongoing rethinking of big ideas, assumptions, prior lessons.
5. Spark meaningful connections with prior learning and personal experiences.
6. Naturally recur, creating opportunities for transfer to other situations.

Here are examples of essential questions, organized by subject area, to spark your thinking and clarify these criteria.

Essential Questions in Social Studies

- Whose story is this? Whose voices aren't we hearing?
- How should governments balance the rights of individuals with the common good?
- Should _____ (e.g., immigration, alcohol and drugs, media) be restricted or regulated? When? Who decides?
- Why do people move? When do they "have to" move and when do they "choose to" move?
- What is worth fighting for? Who decides?

Essential Questions in Mathematics

- What kind of problem is this?
- What should I do when I'm stuck?
- When is estimation better than counting?
- How can I simplify this into a more familiar and easier-to-work-with quantity?
- What is the pattern?
- How does *what* we measure influence *how* we measure? How does *how* we measure influence *what* we measure (or don't measure)?
- How accurate (precise) does this need to be?
- Given _____, what can we conclude? What can't we conclude?

Essential Questions in Language Arts

- What is the relationship between "fiction" and "truth"?
- How are stories from other places and times about me?
- Have we run across this idea before?
- What do good readers do?
- What is the author saying? What makes you think so?
- How do texts differ, and how should I read as a result?
- What should I do when the text doesn't make any sense?
- How do effective writers hook and hold their readers?
- Why am I writing? For whom?

Essential Questions in Art

- What is art? How does it differ from "crafts"?
- Where can we find art?
- What can artworks tell us about a culture or a society? How can they mislead us about that culture or society?
- What's the difference between a thoughtful and a thoughtless critique?
- Do artists have a responsibility to their audiences? Do audiences have a responsibility to artists?

Essential Questions in Science

- What makes objects move the way they do? Why does this thing move that way?
- What are we made of? What is everything made of?
- How are structure and function related in living things? Why is this creature doing this and built like that?
- Where did it go? (with reference to conservation of energy and matter)
- How should we evaluate a scientific claim?
- How can we best measure what we cannot directly see?
- Do the data warrant that otherwise-plausible explanation?
- Is this error an avoidable mistake or inherent in the data?

Essential Questions in World Languages

- What are the key similarities and the differences between [target language] and English?
- How do I get beyond thinking in English?
- What is the best way for me to retain as much language as possible in long-term memory?
- How might the context help me understand words I do not know?
- What should I do when I am stuck?
- How can I sound more like a native speaker?
- How can I keep the conversation going?
- How can I explore and describe cultures without stereotyping them?

Design Tip: Although you might "get" the idea of essential questions, it doesn't follow that you will necessarily be able to immediately transfer your understanding and write great essential questions on your own. Practice makes perfect. You have to keep writing and tinkering, and try your ideas out on colleagues and students; before long you'll have good ones.

Design Task: Brainstorm essential questions based on the big ideas for your unit. Then, check your questions against the criteria for essential questions (the numbered list presented earlier in this module).

Nonessential (but Important to the *Teacher*) Questions

When you step back and self-assess your brainstormed essential questions against the criteria, you may find, alas, that some turn out not to be essential. Even when we try hard to come up with such questions, they can still end up like these: "What is a linear equation?" or "Why is punctuation important?"—even though the briefest self-assessment against the criteria would reveal that such questions are not essential in our sense. The question you came up with may be essential to your teaching, of course, but that isn't what we are looking for here. Typical novice-designer questions are often too leading or knowledge focused.

Here are additional examples of common *non*essential questions we have gleaned from hundreds of sample units:

- What are the elements of a story?
- How does the body turn food into energy?
- Why does the future tense matter?
- What are real-world applications of [a topic]?
- What were the three causes of [any event]?
- Why is it important to be healthy?

We trust that you are starting to see why none of these questions is "essential" in the sense defined earlier. Each question is really just seeking (or pointing to) an "official" and final correct answer instead of setting up an in-depth and often open inquiry or it asks for a list rather than in-depth inquiry. If we as teachers persist in only asking questions to which there is a right answer (a hard habit to break), we will be shortchanging the needed inquiry process at the heart of in-depth understanding.

A different way to make the point is to say that teachers often conflate two meanings of *essential* when first working with such questions: essential to me in my role as a teacher of core content versus essential for students to continuously consider so as to gain insight, make connections, and facilitate transfer of learning. We want more of the latter kinds of questions and fewer of the former in an understanding-focused curriculum.

A slight edit can make a big difference. "Why does grammar matter?" is a teacherly question. We can imagine all the students responding in unison (with less than full enthusiasm) with the "correct" answer. Here's a better version of the original question: "How well and where can you succeed in life speaking *ungram*matically?" You can see by the way that the original question is now posed that we send the message that we will be exploring the value of grammar honestly and openly rather than expecting students to take it as a given. (A simple and elegant further edit to the question might be this: "How much does grammar matter?")

You may want to test your draft essential questions keeping in mind this caution: does the question signal open inquiry, or is it itching to get to a right answer? (See Figure F.1 for additional guidance in distinguishing between essential questions and "knowledge questions.")

Purpose Overrides Format

As the test just mentioned suggests, the purpose of the question matters more than its format. Many teachers new to essential questions tend to think of a question as a device for getting to important answers; in UbD the point of an essential question is to short-circuit knee-jerk thinking and glib answers—to keep important questions alive. In other words, the goal of meaning-making is fundamentally different from the goal of content acquisition—yet teachers and students alike are used to thinking of learning as being about acquisition only. A truly essential question is worth asking—and asking again. Indeed, it is only through ongoing consideration, reflection, and rethinking that in-depth understanding is developed and deepened over time.

This point is concretely underscored on the UbD Template. As noted in Module B, describing the template, we ask you to identify essential questions, not essential answers as a desired result in Stage 1. The point is to keep asking and to get better at asking and considering the key questions.

Thus the format of the question is not really the point; the point is what you do with the question in the unit, what you signal about its purpose. "Is biology destiny?" may sound like it wants a correct yes or no answer; a few pointed and thought-provoking discussions and lessons can quickly signal that the question is designed to sharpen and keep us thinking while studying biology. Conversely, a question that seems open-ended—for example, "When should the United States go to war?"—may sound like we are seeking a genuine inquiry. But if it is simply a

Figure F.1

Distinguishing Essential Questions from Knowledge Questions

Essential Questions	Knowledge Questions
1. Are meant to be explored, argued, and continually revisited (and reflected upon).	1. Have a specific, straightforward, unproblematic answer.
2. Have various plausible answers. Often the answers to these questions raise new questions.	2. Are asked to prompt factual recall rather than to generate a sustained inquiry.
3. Should spark or provoke thought and stimulate students to engage in sustained inquiry and extended thinking.	3. Are more likely to be asked by a teacher or a textbook than by a curious student or person out in the world.
4. Reflect genuine questions that real people seriously ask, either in their work or in their lives—not a "teacherly" question asked only in schools.	4. Are more rhetorical than genuine.

Other Points to Remember

• It is the *purpose* of the question that matters, not its phrasing. How the question is pursued (or not) in the activities and assessments determines if it is "essential." In this regard, many essential questions begin with "open" stems (e.g., *Why…? In what ways…? How might… ?*), but this is not a requirement. Questions may be phrased as if they could be answered with a "yes/no" or a single answer, yet still meet the criteria of "essential" (e.g., *Is biology destiny? What should we eat? Which modern president has the most disappointing legacy?*). In other words, the format or phrasing of the question is not the sole determiner of its purpose.

• Some essential questions are meant to be guiding; that is, they are initially open to many plausible interpretations and answers, but they *eventually* end in an understanding. Many essential questions in the sciences fit this description (e.g., *What are things made of? Where does the water go? Why do things move the way they do?*). Nonetheless, such questions can guide student inquiry, stimulate thinking, and encourage meaning-making by the learner.

• Note the distinction between "hook" questions (e.g., *Can what you eat help prevent zits?*) intended to engage students' interest in a new topic, and essential questions. We recommend placing hook questions in Stage 3 as part of the learning plan.

rhetorical question that points quickly to the "official" teacher or textbook answer, then the question was not really essential in our sense.

Essential Questions and Young Children

You may be thinking that an essential question is fit only for older or advanced students. Not so. Consider the following questions for use with children in the primary grades:

- Which strangers can I trust?
- Why did that "bad" thing (e.g., fight on the playground, accident in the park, thoughtless stealing) happen?
- Why did the author say that?
- Why do people do stupid things?
- What didn't I see there? How can I see better?
- If that's my purpose, how should I speak?
- How can I best show _____ (e.g., the pattern, my ideas)?

Notice that these questions are about ideas and strategies, yet they are cast in a way that is relevant and accessible to young children. These questions, too, lack easy answers—but that doesn't mean children cannot ponder and discuss them fruitfully. Indeed, they *should* be pondering them! Here's a think-aloud example:

> *Which stranger should I trust?* I am lost in this crowded store, and I cannot find my mom; what should I do? I need to get help from a stranger—but which one? Gee, a "trustworthy" stranger—who might *that* be? Oooh, but I was told to be careful and never to talk to or go with strangers. Then what do I do now? I need to ask someone. So which of these strangers *can* I trust—mindful of the danger? Well, someone who works for the store, in store clothes, seems like the most *safe* stranger.

Serious learning always involves inquiry in the face of uncertainty; it is never just about pat answers that obviate the need for thought. We want our children to "know what to do when they don't know what to do," as a teacher once put it to us in a workshop. That requires not rote answers but thoughtful consideration of a vital question over time—figuring out whom you can really trust is a lifelong quest!

In short, a truly essential question is "alive." It typically raises more questions in our attempts to answer it, whether it is asked of 4-year-old kids or 40-year-old adults—even as carefully considering it leads to answers. The goal in working with essential questions is to train students in how to consider such questions without either hurrying to a glib thought-ending answer or giving up in despair.

Note, too, that many of the best essential questions should be asked of people across all age levels and time. Here are examples of such timeless questions:

- Who is my audience, and what follows for what I say and how I say it?
- What should I do when I am stuck?
- How much power should leaders have?
- Which parts of me and my life are fixed, and which parts of me am I free to change?
- Who is a true friend?
- What does it mean to be an American?
- How can I turn this unfamiliar problem into something more familiar and easier to work with?
- What does this (e.g., picture, text, play) mean?
- Why do people move?
- How should I (we) decide?

We refer to such questions as "overarching" in that they transcend any given unit topic and, sometimes, even subject areas. They can fruitfully be asked over and over again. Indeed, spiraling into greater depth using the same question is more likely to develop and deepen understanding than a curriculum that covers hundreds of topics on a single pass.

Essential Questions and Skills Teaching

In our experience, teachers who focus their teaching around concepts (e.g., in literature, social studies, and science) tend to be more comfortable developing and using essential questions. Teachers who focus on skill development (e.g., in mathematics, language arts, physical education, foreign language, and music) may see essential questions as unnatural and unnecessary for much of what they teach and want learned. Indeed, it is not uncommon to hear comments such as this: "Essential questions don't work in my area. We just teach skills; there are no big ideas or issues here."

Not so, we contend—as the earlier example of "space" in sports should suggest. When we are confronted with real challenges or problems, in transfer situations, we must ask questions; for example, Which skill is best used here? What approach is likely to be most efficient and effective here? When should I use this strategy versus that one? How will this audience influence my performance? Strategy and purpose questions are all "essential" ones. And transfer of skill always requires asking strategic questions—questions involving judgments, not facts.

Sometimes, in other words, the essential question in a skill area is not about concepts or theory but practical decision making. Consider a few of Pólya's famous problem-solving questions in mathematics from *How to Solve It*:

- *Have you seen it before?* Or have you seen the same problem in a slightly different form?

- *Do you know a related problem?* Do you know a theorem that could be useful?
- *Here is a problem related to yours and solved before. Could you use it?* (2004, pp. iv–x)

Note that such questions need to go from being teacher prompts to self-prompts. The goal of learning is meaning-making and transfer on our own, and the key questions in literacy, mathematics, and other skill-focused teaching areas involve these kinds of metacognitive prompts when we confront obstacles to performance. Again, that's why we call them essential questions and place them in Stage 1 as a goal: the goal is to become expert in asking the right questions when challenged. (Note also, however, that the questions are essential only if the learner is confronted with a *genuine problem*, as opposed to a simple "plug and chug" exercise with an obvious unknown.) Figure F.2 provides several examples to help you better distinguish skill from thoughtful strategy, and the questions related to skill use.

Admittedly, when first learning a new skill, there may be no decisions to make; the goal may be to simply acquire the skill and develop a degree of proficiency with it. But students quickly understand that there are decisions to be made, hence strategies related to the effective use of that skill. It is in the arena of strategies and contextual decisions that big ideas (and their companion understandings and essential questions) are typically found.

⟳ **Design Task:** Examine the essential questions for your unit in light of the previous discussion. Are there any skill areas for which worthwhile essential questions about strategy and self-prompting can be included?

Perhaps you are still puzzling over essential questions. The exercise in Figure F.3 will help you better understand essential questions, and it also illustrates an effective technique you can use with students to ensure clarity about any challenging idea.

Framing Understandings

Understandings are the specific insights, inferences, or conclusions about the big idea you want your students to leave with. The more enduring the understanding, the more central it should be to unit design. As we noted in Module E, you may find it helpful to think of an understanding as the moral of the story, or rather, of your unit. In UbD, understandings

- Are *full-sentence statements* reflecting conclusions about the content via big ideas—the particulars of what you want students to understand about that idea. For example, "I want learners to understand that a written constitution and encoded rule of law are essential to safeguard the people's rights in a democracy."
- Can be gained only through *guided inference* whereby the learner is helped to make, recognize, or verify a conclusion. They are thus not "teachable"

Figure F.2

Essential Questions for Skill-Related Goals

Subject	Skill	Strategy	Essential Questions
Reading	"Sound out" unfamiliar words.	Use context clues to figure out the word's meaning.	• What's the author trying to say? • How can I find out what these words might mean?
Writing	Follow the five-paragraph essay structure.	Match your word choices with your purpose and audience.	• If that's my purpose and audience, what follows for my writing?
Mathematics	Dividing fractions: Invert and multiply.	Problem solving: • Simplify equivalent expressions. • Work backward from end result.	• How can I turn unknowns into knowns? • What form must this end up in?
Visual Arts/ Graphic Design	Use the color wheel to select complementary colors.	Use colors to reinforce the mood you want to evoke in the viewer.	• What am I trying to make the viewer feel? • How can I best evoke mood using color?
Carpentry	Apply proper techniques when using a band saw.	Measure twice, cut once.	• How can I best save time, money, and energy?

facts. Understandings are inherently abstract, usually not obvious, sometimes counterintuitive, and possibly misunderstood by students, so simply "teaching" the understanding does not guarantee that students will "get" it.

Beginners with UbD often end up mistakenly listing the topic when asked to identify understandings (e.g., "I want students to understand the Civil War") instead of stating what conclusions they want learners to derive or grasp from a study of the war. Thus, as a practical technique, we ask you to use the word *that* in the template—"I want my students to understand that...." So, in our Civil War example, the revised answer would be "I want my students to understand that the war was fought over issues of economic history and states' rights; the morality of slavery was not the sole cause of the war's beginning."

Design Tip: When you get stuck trying to think of how to turn your content standards and objectives into understandings, try these two prompts:

- Those are the facts they must learn, but what do the facts mean?
- If the content of the unit is the story, then what is the moral of the story (in this case, of the unit)?

Figure F.3

What Makes a Question "Essential"?

Part 1: Examine the following essential questions (1–6) and nonexamples (7–12) to determine the common characteristics of essential questions. List the common characteristics.

Essential Questions	Not Essential Questions
1. How are "form" and "function" related in biology? 2. How do effective writers hook and hold their readers? 3. Who "wins" and who "loses" when technologies change? 4. Should it be an axiom if it is not obvious? 5. What distinguishes fluent foreigners from native speakers? 6. How would life be different if we couldn't measure time?	7. How many legs does a spider have? How does an elephant use its trunk? 8. What is "foreshadowing"? Can you find an example of foreshadowing in the story? 9. What is the original meaning of the term *technology* (from its Greek root, *techne*)? 10. By what axioms are we able to prove the Pythagorean theorem? 11. What are some French colloquialisms? 12. How many minutes are in an hour? How many hours are in a day?
Common characteristics of essential questions:	

Part 2: Test your theory about essential questions by deciding which of the following questions (13–18) are essential, using your list of characteristics as criteria. Mark yes if it is an essential question or no if it's not.

	YES	NO
13. What is the relationship between popularity and greatness in literature?	_____	_____
14. When was the Magna Carta signed?	_____	_____
15. Crustaceans—what's up with that?	_____	_____
16. Which U.S. president has the most disappointing legacy?	_____	_____
17. To what extent are common sense and science related?	_____	_____
18. What's the pattern?	_____	_____

Part 3: Review the answer key and explanations; revise your description of essential questions.

13. Yes—Open-ended, thought provoking; supports inquiry, discussion, and debate.
14. No—A fact question with a single "correct" answer.
15. No—Somewhat open, but does not necessarily point toward any important ideas.
16. Yes—Open-ended, thought provoking; supports inquiry, discussion, and debate with follow-up prompts (e.g., Why? What's your reasoning? Support your choice).
17. Yes—Open-ended, thought provoking; supports inquiry and discussion.
18. Maybe—Not an essential question *if* it points to a correct answer (e.g., 1, 2, 4, 8, 14, _____), but could be *if* the students are given complex data with no obvious pattern; in this case, students will need to use reasoning to make and test inferences.

Revised descriptions for common characteristics of essential questions:

Source: © 2004 ASCD. All rights reserved.

Here we list some examples of important meanings in various subject areas. Notice that they are stated as full-sentence generalizations that specify the desired understandings.

Algebra: The aim in algebraic problem solving is to turn unclear relationships of unknowns and unfamiliars into knowns and familiars by means of equivalent statements.

Arithmetic: Different number systems (e.g., bases) and expressions (e.g., fractions) can represent the same quantities. The goal, context, and ease of use determine the best choice.

Art: Great artists often break with established traditions, conventions, and techniques to better express what they see and feel. A confident free society willingly tolerates the turmoil that unorthodox art may cause.

Economics: In a free-market economy, price is a function of supply and demand.

Geography: The topography, climate, and natural resources of a region influence the culture, economy, and lifestyle of its inhabitants ("Geography is destiny").

Literature and Reading: An effective story engages the reader by leaving out key facts and raising questions—tensions, mystery, dilemmas, or uncertainty—about what will happen next.

Mathematics: The needed approach and precision vary by situation. Mathematical models have the power to illuminate complex phenomena—but also the possibility of distorting their meaning.

Music: Popular music has shifted from emphasizing melody to emphasizing multilayered rhythms ("It don't mean a thing if it ain't got that swing").

Physical Education: Unpredictable movement—in pace and direction—is key to good offense. Creating "space" away from the ball is just one way to increase scoring opportunities (in soccer, football, field hockey, basketball, and other sports).

Science: Correlation does not mean or ensure causality.

World Language: Translation rarely involves a one-to-one correspondence of words. Many words and expressions are idiomatic. Just because you can translate each word doesn't mean you will understand the speaker.

Writing: Self-deprecating humor can be an effective (and ironic) way to persuade audiences.

As with essential questions, some understandings are more encompassing than others. Sometimes the inferences we want students to draw are closely tied to unit content. At other times, we want them to make and see the power of broad generalizations.

⟳ **Design Tip:** If you get stuck trying to think of understandings that you want students to attain, think about the opposite—that is, overcoming the misunderstandings that are predictable or typical. Sometimes it is easier to think of specific misunderstandings that students have rather than the understandings you want them to achieve.

Understandings Versus Truisms

So, you have come up with a full-sentence generalization related to your unit topic. Unfortunately, that doesn't guarantee that you have identified a genuine understanding worth learning. Just as some essential questions are really too "teacherly," it is common for novice designers to identify vague notions, truisms, or facts they want learned instead of understandings. What do we mean by vague notion or truism? Look at these examples:

- History is about the rise and fall of peoples and cultures over time.
- Things fall or move in predictable ways.
- Math involves patterns.
- Good readers read nonfiction carefully.

Do you see what these examples all have in common? They are either so vague or obvious as to be unhelpful for designing units or helping students learn. In one sense, there is no "understanding" to arrive at: Most students already know these things. Rather, the aim in framing understandings is to identify the hard-won insights that can come only from digging into the content and drawing important conclusions from it. Here, then, are the same truisms rewritten to suggest what a genuine understanding is:

- History is always written by the winners, making it difficult to understand the "real" story of all peoples and cultures.
- $F = ma$
- Seemingly random data often reflect elegant functional relationships.
- Good readers approach a nonfiction text with just the right mix of respect for the author's argument and skepticism about its truth.

Note that the teacher has a much clearer direction for what to stress and teach in each unit based on these edits. And note, too, this paradox: *Understandings eventually become "facts" in our minds; many things we call "facts" are actually now-familiar understandings.*

If you teach very young or inexperienced students, you may have quarreled with our calling the first set of statements obvious. "None of those four original ideas is obvious to a 5-year-old! They are only obvious to teenagers and older students!" You may well be correct. This is what makes teaching for understanding so much more challenging than teaching for content acquisition. A person either has the knowledge and skill or he doesn't. But understanding takes place along a developmental continuum over time, once hard-won insights become familiar, working knowledge.

On the other hand, we would still claim that those "understandings" are too vague for students—especially younger students. "Good readers read carefully"— what does that really mean? What should one do to be a more careful reader? The teacher could say this over and over, and it would not provide young readers with any insight into how to be more careful. The best understandings are written to help teachers and students know the specific insights the unit is meant to achieve. By definition, students don't start out understanding the understanding! They may not even know what the understanding means when they actually hear it or read it. That's the point of the unit: to help the student come to understand it.

Understandings and Skill

As we noted with essential questions, it is a misconception to think that there are no big ideas in skill-focused teaching. In subjects such as reading, writing, mathematics, world languages, vocational courses, physical education, and others that emphasize skill development, the understandings can be typically found in the strategies, rationale, or value of the skills. For example, here's a skill-based understanding for sports skills (e.g., throwing a baseball or football, swinging a golf club, throwing darts, etc.): "When you 'follow through' (in your throw or stroke), you will generate greater power and control." Such an understanding enables students to practice the skill (being mindful of following through) while monitoring its effects. Just as coaches and teachers encourage such "mindful" practice in athletics, teachers can similarly cultivate skill-based understandings in academic areas.

Design Tip: In skill areas the understandings most often reflect the *rationale* for a strategy and thus generalize about best practice. Take a strategy—for example, "Keep your eye on the ball"—and provide the rationale for it: "Most athletes lose eye contact when they swing. You need to keep your eye on the ball by taking deliberate action to be looking at it all through your swing."

Still puzzled over understandings? Figure F.4 is another exercise that should help you.

Design Task: Examine the understandings for your unit in light of the previous discussion and design tips. How might your understandings be edited to best summarize the important inferences that you want students to make and the insights you hope they will attain?

Figure F.4

Framing Understandings

Part 1: Examine the following examples (1–5) and nonexamples (6–10) to determine the common characteristics of an effectively framed understanding. List these below.

Enduring Understandings	Not Enduring Understandings
The student will understand that...	*The student will understand...*
1. In a free-market economy, price is a function of supply and demand.	6. That the price of long-distance phone calls has declined during the past decade.
2. True friendship is revealed during difficult times, not happy times.	7. True friendship.
3. Statistical analysis and data display often reveal patterns that may not be obvious.	8. Mean, median, and mode are measures of central tendency.
4. The most efficient and effective stroke mechanics in swimming involve pushing the maximum amount of water directly backward.	9. That they should not cup their hands when swimming the freestyle.
5. Heating of the Earth's surface and atmosphere by the sun drives convection within the atmosphere and oceans, producing winds and ocean currents.	10. Wind is a force of nature.

Common characteristics of enduring understandings:

Part 2: Use your list of characteristics as criteria to determine which of the following examples are effectively framed as enduring understandings. Mark yes if it is an enduring understanding or no if it's not.

	YES	NO
11. The concept of estivation.	___	___
12. The USDA Food Pyramid presents relative, not absolute, guidelines for a balanced diet.	___	___
13. Mathematical models simplify reality to enable useful solutions.	___	___
14. How to tell time.	___	___
15. The causes and effects of the Civil War.	___	___
16. That the Magna Carta was signed on June 15, 1215.	___	___

Part 3: Review the answer key and explanations; revise your description of enduring understandings.

11. No—States the concept to be learned, not the understanding about the concept that should be learned.
12. Yes—The word 'relative' in this statement signals that there is not a single prescribed or pat formula for healthy eating, given individual and cultural differences.
13. Yes—This is a transferable idea, applicable throughout school and life. And it is not obvious that insightful models greatly simplify reality at some potential cost, despite their power.
14. No—Skill objective does not state understandings about telling time that need to be grasped.
15. No—States the topic, not the unobvious understandings about the causes and effects to be achieved.
16. No—States a fact, not an idea.

Refined common characteristics of enduring understandings:

Self-Assessment—Review Criteria for Module F

Self-assess your current unit design against the following criteria:

- Is the content of the unit framed around transferable big ideas (e.g., concepts, themes, issues/debates, processes, problems, challenges, theories, assumptions)?
- Are all the identified essential questions open-ended? Likely to provoke thought and inquiry? Pointing toward important understandings?
- Are the identified understandings based upon transferable big ideas?
- Are the desired understandings stated as full-sentence generalizations in response to the stem "Students will understand that…"?
- Are all of the Stage 1 elements (established goals, understandings, transfer goals, essential questions, knowledge and skills) appropriately connected?

The Nutrition Unit Revisited

We conclude this module by returning to the nutrition unit and viewing refinements to Stage 1. Notice in Figure F.5 (p. 88) that the understandings have been framed as full-sentence generalizations, along with predictable student misconceptions. Companion essential questions are included.

Online you'll find worksheets to help you develop your unit's big ideas, understandings, and essential questions: Figure F.6, Brainstorming Big Ideas; Figure F.7, Brainstorming Essential Questions; Figure F.8, From Topics to Big Ideas; Figure F.9, Manifestations of Big Ideas; Figure F.10, Finding the Big Ideas in Skills; Figure F.11, Example of Essential Questions in Skill Areas; Figure F.12, Identifying Understandings; and Figure F.13, From Skills to Ideas to Understandings.

Further Information on the Ideas and Issues in This Module

Understanding by Design: Professional Development Workbook (McTighe & Wiggins, 2004). Characteristics of essential questions, page 91; examples of essential questions in various subject areas, pages 93–103; essential questions and skills, pages 104–105; Tips for Using Essential Questions, page 106; additional examples of understandings ("meanings"), pages 108–110; understandings in skill areas, page 118.

Understanding by Design, 2nd ed. (Wiggins & McTighe, 2005). Chapters 5 and 6 have extended discussions of big ideas, understandings, and essential questions.

Schooling by Design: Mission, Action, and Achievement (Wiggins & McTighe, 2007). Chapter 3 has additional examples of overarching understandings and essential questions.

References

Bruner, J. (1960). *The process of education*. Cambridge, MA: Harvard University Press.

McTighe, J., & Wiggins, G. (2004). *Understanding by design: Professional development workbook*. Alexandria, VA: ASCD.

Pólya, G. (2004). *How to solve it: A new aspect of mathematical method* (Expanded ed.). Princeton, NJ: Princeton University Press.

Wiggins, G., & McTighe, J. (2005). *Understanding by design* (2nd ed.). Alexandria, VA: ASCD.

Wiggins, G., & McTighe, J. (2007). *Schooling by design: Mission, action, and achievement*. Alexandria, VA: ASCD.

Figure F.5

Nutrition Unit with Expanded Understandings and Essential Questions

Unit Topic: Nutrition

Subject(s): Health

Grade(s): 5–7

Time Frame: 3 weeks

Stage 1—Desired Results

Understandings

Students will understand that...

• Eating a balanced diet promotes physical and mental health, and enhances one's appearance and energy level. Poor nutrition leads to a variety of health problems. (*Related misconception: If food is good for you, it must taste bad.*)

• Healthful eating requires an individual to act on available information about nutritious diets, even if it means breaking comfortable habits. (*Related misconception: As long as I'm thin, it doesn't matter what I eat.*)

• The USDA Food Pyramid defines healthy eating, but healthy eating varies for each individual depending upon age, lifestyle, culture, and available foods. (*Related misconception: Everyone must follow the same prescription for good eating.*)

Essential Questions

• What is healthful eating?

• Are you a healthful eater? How will you know?

• How could a healthy diet for one person be unhealthy for another?

• Why are there so many health problems caused by poor nutrition despite all of the available information about healthful eating?

Module G

Determining Evidence of Understanding and Developing Assessment Tasks

Purpose: Determine valid evidence of the understanding goals and develop assessment task ideas using the six facets of understanding.

Desired Results: Unit designers will understand that

- Understanding is revealed through six facets of understanding: explanation, interpretation, application, perspective, empathy, and self-knowledge.

- These six facets give rise to interesting and useful approaches to assessment.

Unit designers will be able to

- Develop evidence needed for their understanding-related unit goals—transfer and meaning—using the six facets of understanding.

The end product will be a more refined unit plan, including assessments of the understanding goals of Stage 1.

You should work on Module G if you feel the need or desire to think further about assessment of your understanding-related goals.

You can skip Module G if you are familiar with the six facets of understanding or know how to design valid assessments of understanding.

In Module E, we asked you to consider in detail the four kinds of learning goals for Stage 1: knowledge (K), skill (S), understanding (U), and transfer (T). In this module, we focus on the two understanding goals and take a finer-grained look at the assessment evidence they require in Stage 2.

Evidence of Understanding

Recall the basic logic of the first two stages of backward design in UbD:

- What are the desired results?
- If those are the desired results, what follows for assessment?

As previously noted, when understanding is our goal, we need evidence that the students have successfully made meaning of the content (e.g., can draw sound inferences or make valid connections and explain these), as opposed to merely recalling something that the teacher or textbook said. Moreover, we are looking for the ability of learners to transfer prior learning to new or novel-looking tasks or settings, with minimal or no prompting from the test or the teacher. Both abilities require learners to also be able to continually address essential questions.

To be a valid test of understanding, then, success at the tasks or tests we design must depend primarily upon the depth of the understanding a student has, as opposed to mere facility with words, good recall, creation of a nice product, or skill in performing in front of others. In other words, as assessors we must be clear about the essential indicators of understanding and not be swayed by tangential qualities of performance or surface features of student work.

The following prompts (corresponding to the contrast just made) indicate the challenge ahead:

- Yes, the student is articulate and offers many facts, but is her argument logical and grounded in the content of the unit on World War II?
- Unfortunately, he forgets some details in *Charlotte's Web*, but doesn't he grasp the importance and consequences of the themes of friendship and motive?
- Yes, his rap was skillful and entertaining, but does the rap provide any solid evidence of understanding of *Winn Dixie*—the text it was supposedly based on?
- Alas, she produced a messy and poorly built Rube Goldberg–like machine, but doesn't her corresponding explanation of the physics nonetheless demonstrate genuine insight into the relevant principles?

Our point is not that features such as factual recall and oral proficiency should never count. Rather, because the goal is understanding, assessment should focus on it—even if we also want to give feedback on work quality, accuracy, and other elements.

You will recall our two-question test of validity in Module D: Could the student do the performance but not understand? And vice versa: Could the student do poorly at the specific test but still be said to understand based on other evidence? In Figure G.1 we offer a more comprehensive test of your tests, based on the ideas of this module.

Figure G.1

Applying the Two-Question Validity Test

Purpose: To apply the two-question validity test to your assessments.

Directions: Test your unit assessments using the following question prompts.

Stage 1 Desired Results:			
Stage 2 Evidence:			
	Very likely*	**Somewhat likely**	**Very unlikely**
1. How likely is it that a student could do well on the assessment by			
• Making clever guesses, parroting back, or "plugging in" what was learned, perhaps with accurate recall but limited or no understanding?			
• Making a good-faith effort, with lots of hard work and enthusiasm, but with limited understanding?			
• Producing a lovely product or an engaging and articulate performance, but with limited understanding?			
2. How likely is it that a student could do poorly on the assessment by			
• Failing to meet the requirements of this particular task while nonetheless revealing a good understanding of the ideas?			
• Not being skilled at certain aspects of the task, but those skills are *not* central to the goal or involve outside learning or natural talent (e.g., require acting or computer ability unrelated to Stage 1 goals)?			

*"Very likely" means that the assessment is not aligned with goal(s).

Source: © 2004 ASCD. All rights reserved.

Assessing understanding is thus harder than just making up a quiz to check for recall of facts or isolated skill proficiency (i.e., acquisition). There is always the danger that the different variables at work in performance might confuse or mislead us as to what the student truly understands. It's no wonder, then, that teachers and measurement specialists have long been drawn to simpler test items that isolate discrete knowledge and skills because these are quicker, cheaper, and less controversial to design, administer, and score. In general, however, such assessments cannot provide sufficient and compelling evidence of genuine understanding.

Assessments of Transfer

Common sense suggests that the ultimate test of genuine understanding concerns the ability to transfer: What can learners do with what they have learned in school? Although meaning-making is, of course, necessary, it is arguably not sufficient; transfer is our focus as educators. Learners have to be able not just to think well but to act effectively on their ideas, skill, and knowledge. That's why we place transfer at the top of Stage 1 and highlight transfer tasks in Stage 2.

But transfer doesn't mean just plugging content into a well-known format, pat problem, or familiar exercise. A valid assessment of transfer ability requires two elements not found in mere recall: a novel look and feel to the task, and a context that requires students to tailor prior learning to a concrete situation. Finally, students must be able to make these judgments and applications independently, as we discussed briefly in Module D.

This is not a new or controversial idea. Bloom and colleagues (1956) made this point more than 50 years ago in the taxonomy:

> If the situations... are to involve application as we are defining it here, then they must either be situations new to the student or situations containing new elements as compared to the situation in which the abstraction was learned.... Ideally we are seeking a problem which will test the extent to which an individual has learned to apply the abstraction in a practical way. (p. 125)

Note two phrases that highlight the demands of genuine transfer versus mere plugging in: we are seeking a problem cast in *situations new to the student*, and a task that will test the extent to which the student has learned to apply an *abstraction in a practical way*. Having learned a concept, formula, method, principle, theory, or strategy (out of context, as an abstraction), we need to find out if students can use it effectively, in a specific, unfamiliar-looking but ultimately manageable context—with minimal teacher guidance.

Here are some examples of such transfer tasks related to abstract ideas:

- Use your writing skills (a general repertoire) to develop a persuasive letter to your parents asking for more allowance (a specific task, purpose, and audience).
- Use your understanding of Newton's laws of motion (abstract ideas) to design an exciting yet safe amusement park ride and explain the various forces involved (specific task).
- Develop an equation and graphic representation (general mathematical knowledge) to compare pricing for various cell phone calling plans (specific data in context).
- Use your understanding of the word *friend* (general concept) to determine if Frog and Toad are always acting like true friends in the stories (specific situations).

As you think about assessing understanding in Stage 2, it is vital to design assessments backward from the goal of transfer (and meaning), not mere content mastery. You may want to look back at your original answers to the "purpose" questions about your unit in Modules D through F for ideas about transfer tasks because such goals suggest them. You may also wish to edit your transfer goals in light of the discussion so far.

Six Facets of Understanding

Transfer manifests itself in a variety of ways. More specifically, we propose that understanding as transfer is revealed through six facets of understanding, summarized here. Individuals who understand and can transfer their learning

- Can *explain*: make connections, draw inferences, express them in their *own* words with support or justification; use apt analogies; teach others.
- Can *interpret*: make sense of, provide a revealing historical or personal dimension to ideas, data, and events; make it personal or accessible through images, anecdotes, analogies, and stories; turn data into information; provide a compelling and coherent theory.
- Can *apply and adjust*: use what they have learned in varied and unique situations; go beyond the context in which they learned to new units, courses, and situations beyond the school.
- Have *perspective*: see the big picture; are aware of, and consider, various points of view; take a critical or disinterested stance; recognize and avoid bias in how positions are stated.
- Show *empathy*: perceive sensitively; can "walk in another's shoes"; find potential value in what others might find odd, alien, or implausible.
- Have *self-knowledge*: show metacognitive awareness; reflect on the meaning of new learning and experiences; recognize the prejudices, projections, and

habits of mind that both shape and impede their own understanding; are aware of what they do not understand in this context.

We do not intend that the six facets represent a theory of how people come to understand something. Instead, the facets are intended to serve as six helpful lenses or indicators of how understanding is often revealed in action—in performance, products, words, or behavior. Thus they provide practical frames for the kinds of assessments we might construct to determine the extent and depth of student understanding.

Using the Six Facets

To illustrate how the facets can suggest ideas for assessment, review the examples in Figure G.2. Figure G.3 helpfully places the six facets into a horizontal version of the first two stages of backward design, showing how assessments might be determined, mindful of the facets and the Stage 1 goals. You'll find additional prompts and ideas for using the facets in Figures G.4 and G.5.

It is important to understand that the goal here is not necessarily to have an assessment task for all six facets. Indeed, not every facet is well suited to every understanding. Nor is there a quota: quality is not quantity. The facets are simply provided to help spark suitable assessment ideas. In reality, you might end up using only one or two of the listed ideas in your unit assessments. Nonetheless, many teachers have found that they come up with worthwhile ideas when considering the six facets. For example, in Figure G.5, the fourth verb listed under "Application" is *debug*. Here is an assessment task based on that idea:

> Alberto wanted to decide which of two spot removers is best. First he tried Spot Remover A on a T-shirt that had fruit stains and chocolate stains. Next he tried Spot Remover B on jeans that had grass stains and rust stains. Then he compared the results.
>
> *Explain:* What did Alberto do wrong that will make it hard for him to know which spot remover is best? How should he change his experiment?

Misconception Alert

Here are two common misconceptions about the six facets of understanding and their use.

1. *The six facets are listed in a hierarchy, like Bloom's Taxonomy.* Not so. The six facets of understanding were conceived as six equal and hopefully suggestive indicators of understanding and thus are used to develop or select assessment tasks and prompts. They were never intended to be a hierarchy.

2. *We must use all six facets when assessing understanding.* No. Designers should select the appropriate facet or facets depending on the nature of the content and

Figure G.2

Performance Task Ideas Based on the Six Facets

Facets / Subject	Explanation	Interpretation	Application	Perspective	Empathy	Self-Knowledge
History/ Social Studies	Provide conceptual clarification (e.g., "freedom" compared to "license"; meaning of the term "third world").	Develop an oral history on the significance of the 1960s using primary sources, and write a historical biography.	Design a museum exhibit on the causes and effects of early 20th century immigration.	Compare British and French textbook accounts of the Revolutionary War with your textbook account.	Role-play a meeting of the minds (e.g., Truman deciding to drop the atomic bomb).	Self-assess your involvement in class discussions and performances, and explain your patterns of participation.
Mathematics	Study a common phenomenon (e.g., weather data). Reveal subtle and easily overlooked patterns in the data.	Do a trend analysis of a finite data set.	Develop a new statistic for evaluating the value of a baseball player in key situations.	Examine the differences when using various measures (e.g., mean, median) for calculating grades.	Read *Flatland* and a set of letters between mathematicians explaining why they fear publishing their findings; write a reflective essay on the difficulty of explaining new ideas, even "abstract" ones.	Develop a mathematical résumé with a brief description of your intellectual strengths and weaknesses.
English/ Language Arts	Describe why a particular rhetorical technique is effective in a speech.	"What's wrong with Holden?" Make sense of the main character in *Catcher in the Rye.*	What makes a "great book"? Make an audiotape review of a favorite book for the school library.	Read and discuss *The Real Story of the Three Little Pigs* by A. Wolf.	Work in a soup kitchen, read a book by Charles Dickens, and write an essay on the experiences of the homeless.	Attach a self-assessment to each paper you write reflecting on *your* writing process.
Arts	Explain the role of silence in music.	Represent fear and hope in a visual collage or dance.	Write and perform a one-act play on a school issue.	Critique three different versions of the same Shakespeare play (focus on a key scene).	Imagine you are Juliet in *Romeo and Juliet,* and consider your terrible, final act. What are you thinking and feeling?	Keep a log of the drama class exercises that demand the most from you emotionally.
Science	Link everyday actions and facts to the laws of physics, concentrating on easily misunderstood aspects (e.g., mass compared to weight).	Take readings of pond water to determine whether the algae problem is serious.	Perform a chemical analysis of local stream water to monitor EPA compliance, and present findings.	Conduct thought experiments (e.g., Einstein's "What would the world be like if I were riding on a beam of light?").	Read and discuss premodern or discredited scientific writings to identify plausible or "logical" theories (given the information available at the time).	Propose solutions to an ineffective cooperative learning activity based on what didn't work in your group.

the desired understandings about it. For example, *interpretation* and *empathy* are appropriate facets to use in assessing students' understanding of a novel, whereas *application* and *explanation* fit naturally in mathematics.

⮎ **Design Task:** Examine the understanding goals you've identified for your unit and see how they might be better assessed using one or more of the six facets.

⮎ **Design Tip:** Have fun with the six facets. Because they represent neither a hierarchy nor a quota, you don't have to address all or most of them. They simply represent interesting possibilities for the design of understanding-focused performance tasks. Don't force it—for example, by trying to create an "empathy" task in mathematics. However, one chemistry teacher did come up with the following task idea by considering empathy: *Write an obituary for the death of an element in which you explain the effects of losing this element.*

Tasks and indicators. Once we start to think through what counts as appropriate evidence of goals, we also realize that there are two related but *different* questions being asked in Stage 2:

1. What specific performance should students be able to do well, if the learning has been successful? In other words, what would be valid assessment tasks, questions, or challenges to find out if our teaching goals were met?

2. What would we have to see in order to say that the goals were achieved—regardless of the specifics of the item, question, task, or type of performance? Where should we look and what should we look for in student products and performances—regardless of the test particulars—to determine success or failure at meeting the goals?

These two questions are reflected in the UbD Template. In Stage 2 you are asked to consider the tasks that will provide evidence of Stage 1 goals (Question 1 above), and the criteria by which we look at (any) evidence related to a Stage 1 goal (Question 2 above). Once we clarify what we are looking for, the answer will be embodied in scoring rubrics and checklists. (We will have more to say about criteria, indicators, and rubrics in later modules.)

Assessing for Transfer Means Assessing for Autonomy

If transfer is the goal, then learners must be expected to (eventually) be able to use knowledge, skill, and understanding on their own. In a word, we always aim as teachers for autonomy—self-regulation and independence from teachers. That means we have to assess backward from self-regulated performance, over time. "My goal as your teacher is to make myself eventually unneeded" is how one teacher explains her role to her students.

Think of sports. The goal is to play the game well, on your own, with the coach on the sideline. And so practice is always designed mindful of the game, and

Figure G.3

Generating Assessment Ideas Using the Facets

Stage 1	Stage 2	
If the desired result is for learners to... →	**then you need evidence of the student's ability to...** →	**so the assessments need to require something like...**
Understand that	**Explain** why similar items might command very different prices based on supply/demand.	• Provide an oral/written explanation of why prices of specific items vary (e.g., ski-lift tickets) as a function of supply and demand.
• Price is a function of supply and demand.	**Interpret** data on prices (e.g., changes in prices for the same item over time).	• Develop a PowerPoint presentation to explain fluctuations in prices over time (e.g., for gasoline or housing).
	Apply, by setting the right prices for items to be sold.	• Conduct consumer research to establish prices for a school store or a fund-raiser.
And thoughtfully consider the question(s) • What determines how much something costs? • What's a "good" price?	**See from the points of view of** buyers and sellers of the same commodity.	• Role-play a buyer-seller negotiation at a flea market, at a garage sale, or on eBay to illustrate different perspectives on price.
	Empathize with the inventor of a new product, trying to set a price; a buyer who has been "taken."	• Write a simulated journal entry as a (consumer, inventor, merchant, etc.) to reveal that person's thoughts and feelings regarding transactions.
	Overcome the naïve or biased idea that commodities have an inherent value or fixed price. **Reflect on** the influence of "sale prices" on your buying habits.	• Describe a specific case in which you (or someone else) came to understand that commodities do not have an inherent value or fixed price.

there are constant formative assessments, in scrimmages and games, of your ability to perform increasingly independently with understanding. Our role as designers of assessment, therefore, is to design assessments that, over time, provide less and less prompting, scaffolding, hints, and reminders; our assessments should require students to increasingly self-direct, self-monitor, and self-adjust performance on their own.

Textbook Assessments

Our discussion of meaning-making and transfer should lead you to wonder about the appropriateness of many assessments provided in textbooks. How much of what is in your textbook can you use as is, and how much of your unit (especially with understanding-related goals) has to be developed apart from the textbook, given your particular goals and context?

Take a minute to scan any relevant textbook chapters for assessments related to one unit that you are teaching now. Given your desired results, and given the assessment implications of those goals, what can be found in the textbook to use as appropriate assessments—that is, appropriate to your specific Stage 1 goal elements?

⤶ Design Tip: Most textbook assessments emphasize discrete knowledge and skill goals. Rarely do textbook assessments honor higher-level, inferential understanding-focused goals—even if they glibly state that the task or question requires "critical thinking" or "analysis." Even rarer are assessments that ask students to make connections across chapters and topics, though such generalizations and comparisons and contrasts are at the heart of real understanding.

Self-Assessment—Review Criteria for Module G

Review your current unit sketch against the following self-assessment questions. Do the assessments of understanding

- Require autonomous transfer to new situations?
- Reflect one or more of the six facets of understanding?

Revise your unit design as needed.

The Nutrition Unit Revisited

Figure G.6 shows how the six facets might be used to generate ideas for assessment tasks for the nutrition unit described in earlier modules.

⤶ For more help in using the six facets of understanding and developing assessment tasks, see the following online worksheets: Figure G.7, Developing Assessment Ideas Using the Six Facets; Figure G.8, What My Transfer Goals Imply for Tasks; and Figure G.9, Analyzing Textbooks and Instructional Resources.

Further Information on the Ideas and Issues in This Module

Understanding by Design, 2nd ed. (Wiggins & McTighe, 2005). Chapter 4, "The Six Facets of Understanding." The goal of transfer is covered in various places, including pages 78–80.

Understanding by Design: Professional Development Workbook (McTighe & Wiggins, 2004). Pages 155–172 and 197–206 provide many tools and exercises on the six facets and the design of relevant performance tasks.

Figure G.4

Six-Facet Question Starters

Explanation

• What is the key idea in _____?
• What are examples of _____?
• What are the characteristics/parts of _____?
• How did this come about? Why is this so? _____
• What caused _____? What are the effects of _____?
• How might we prove/confirm/justify _____?
• How is _____ connected to _____?
• What might happen if _____?
• What are common misconceptions about _____?

Interpretation

• What is the meaning of _____?
• What are the implications of _____?
• What does _____ reveal about _____?
• How is _____ like _____ (analogy/metaphor)?
• How does _____ relate to me/us?
• So what? Why does it matter? _____

Application

• How and when can we use this _____ (knowledge/process)?
• How is _____ applied in the larger world?
• How might _____ help us to _____?
• How could we use _____ to overcome _____?

Perspective

• What are different points of view about _____?
• How might this look from _____'s perspective?
• How is _____ similar to/different from _____?
• What are other possible reactions to _____?
• What are the strengths and weaknesses of _____?
• What are the limits of _____?
• What is the evidence for _____?
• Is the evidence reliable? Sufficient? _____

Empathy

• What would it be like to walk in _____'s shoes?
• How might _____ feel about _____?
• How might we reach an understanding about _____?
• What was _____ trying to make us feel/see?

Self-Knowledge

• How do I know _____?
• What are the limits of my knowledge about _____?
• What are my "blind spots" about _____?
• How can I best show _____?
• How are my views about _____ shaped by _____ (experiences, habits, prejudices, style)?
• What are my strengths and weaknesses in _____?

Source: © 2004 ASCD. All rights reserved.

Schooling by Design: Mission, Action, and Achievement (Wiggins & McTighe, 2007). Chapter 2 discuses the goal of transfer, the difference between the "drill" and the "game," and the nature of genuine accomplishment as a basis for curriculum design. Chapter 3 discusses the need to frame curriculum around the key ("cornerstone") tasks at the heart of every subject area in light of the goal of transfer.

References

Bloom, B. (Ed.). (1956). *Taxonomy of educational objectives, handbook 1: Cognitive domain.* Chicago: University of Chicago Press.

McTighe, J., & Wiggins, G. (2004). *Understanding by design: Professional development workbook.* Alexandria, VA: ASCD.

Wiggins, G., & McTighe, J. (2005). *Understanding by design* (2nd ed.). Alexandria, VA: ASCD.

Wiggins, G., & McTighe, J. (2007). *Schooling by design: Mission, action, and achievement.* Alexandria, VA: ASCD.

Figure G.5

Performance Verbs Related to the Six Facets of Understanding

Use one or more of the following performance verbs to generate ideas for performance tasks and learning events.

Explanation	Interpretation	Application	Perspective	Empathy	Self-Knowledge
demonstrate	create analogies	adapt	analyze	be like	be aware of
derive	critique	build	argue	be open to	realize
describe	document	create	compare	believe	recognize
design	evaluate	debug	contrast	consider	reflect
exhibit	illustrate	decide	criticize	imagine	self-assess
express	judge	design	infer	relate	
induce	make meaning of	exhibit		role-play	
instruct		invent			
justify	make sense of	perform			
model	provide metaphors	produce			
predict	read between the lines	propose			
prove		solve			
show	represent	test			
synthesize	tell a story of	use			
teach	translate				

Figure G.6

Brainstorming Tasks Using the Six Facets

Goals	Six Facets of Understanding	Ideas for Possible Assessment Tasks
Understand the relationship between a balanced diet and physical and mental health.	Explain	Develop a brochure to help people understand what is meant by a "balanced" diet and health problems related to poor nutrition.
Understand the USDA Food Pyramid and how dietary requirements vary for individuals based on age, activity level, weight, and overall health.	Interpret	Discuss: What does the popularity of "fast foods" say about modern life?
Analyze various diets to determine their nutritional values.	Apply	Plan a menu for a class party consisting of healthy yet tasty snacks.
Plan meals that are balanced yet tasty.	Shift perspective	Conduct research to find out if the Food Pyramid guidelines apply in other regions (e.g., Antarctica, Asia, the Middle East) and the effect of diverse diets on health.
Evaluate their own eating patterns and develop a plan for more healthful eating.	Show empathy	Describe how it might feel to live with a dietary restriction due to a medical condition.
	Demonstrate self-knowledge	Reflect on your eating habits. To what extent are you a healthy eater? How might you become a healthier eater?

Source: © 2004 ASCD. All rights reserved.

Module H

Learning for Understanding

Purpose: Refine the learning plan (Stage 3) to help students *acquire* targeted knowledge and skills, make *meaning* of big ideas, and effectively *transfer* their learning in the future.

Desired Results: Unit designers will understand that

- There are three distinct kinds of learning—acquisition (A), meaning (M), and transfer (T)—and the Stage 3 learning plan should appropriately address each.

- The roles of teachers and students vary according to the A-M-T goals.

- Acquisition of knowledge and of skill is not the long-term goal but the means to understanding and transfer ability.

Unit designers will be able to

- Refine their unit by developing a learning plan that reflects meaning and transfer as the ends, and content knowledge and skill as the means.

- Identify appropriate instruction and learning events for the various A-M-T goals.

You should work on Module H if you have not yet developed a learning plan that appropriately addresses the three distinct learning goals of acquisition, meaning, and transfer.

You can skim or skip Module H if you have already developed a learning plan that appropriately addresses the three distinct learning goals of acquisition, meaning, and transfer.

In Stage 1, the UbD Template asks unit designers to identify different types of "desired results"—transfer, meaning, knowledge, and skill—that reference established goals. Now in Stage 3, it is time to consider the different kinds of teaching and learning that are needed, given these goals.

The three types of learning—acquisition, meaning-making, and transfer—reflect noteworthy distinctions that will directly affect the learning plan:

1. Acquisition: Facts and skills are apprehended and acquired. We learn each in turn, either through direct instruction or self-learning. A key benchmark in such learning is automaticity. The student should as soon as possible be able to recall information (e.g., multiplication tables) and perform a skill (e.g., decoding words) on cue, "unthinkingly."

Teaching for knowledge and skill acquisition involves familiar methods of direct instruction—lecture, presentation, advance/graphic organizers, convergent questioning, and demonstration/modeling. The learner's role involves attentiveness, lots of practice, and rehearsal.

2. Meaning: The achievement of meaning involves active intellectual work by the learner to make sense of the content and its implications. The learner must try to understand something that cannot be grasped immediately, by making inferences, forming and testing a theory, looking for connections and patterns *make meaning*. Meaning is not so much "taught and learned" as "challenged and constructed." We *make* meaning.

What are the implications for instruction? Because the meaning of abstract ideas must be ultimately considered and tested in the mind of the learner, a teacher cannot simply transmit insight. Students have to be presented with questions and intellectual tasks that resist an easy answer and demand thought. *What does this passage in the text mean? It could mean a few different things. What kind of problem is this and how should I proceed?* They have to thus be helped to develop mental strategies for building, testing, explaining, and supporting the meanings they make; and develop the habits of mind needed for persisting in the face of challenge and ambiguity.

3. Transfer: The ability to transfer is different from meaning-making, though clearly related to it. Having acquired knowledge and skill, and having been helped to come to understand what the learning means, the learner must now effectively *apply and adapt* this learning to new and particular situations. *I know how to read; how should I read this text? I know how to add and subtract; which operations are needed here? How precise does my answer need to be in this situation? I know how to write essays; how should this particular audience, purpose, deadline, and word limit be addressed?*

What, then, is the role of a teacher when transfer is the goal? A teacher must function like a coach who trains, watches, and offers feedback on performance in athletics and the arts. The learner needs many models and opportunities to try to perform—to apply the learning in new and varied situations. The coach, having modeled different approaches, primarily observes student performance attempts and provides timely and ongoing feedback and advice—while also prompting the performer to reflect on what worked and what didn't and why. Of course, the ultimate goal of transfer is to make the coach barely needed. Therefore, over time, teacher support and scaffolding is gradually removed so that students learn to transfer learning (and process the feedback) on their own. Thus, although there is a role for "teaching"—direct instruction and modeling—it is always in the context of trying to improve (increasingly autonomous) student performance on worthy tasks; it should never leave the student dependent upon the teacher for hints, reminders, and tools. A summary of general teaching approaches related to the goals of acquisition, meaning-making, and transfer appears in Figure H.1.

A related way of considering the teaching and learning implications of the A-M-T goals is to use action verbs to frame what the learner needs to do (and what learning events need to evoke) in order to acquire and understand. Figure H.2 presents a list of such verbs. From the chart we can say in sum that the teacher's job (guided by the unit design) is to help students learn, practice, and master the abilities suggested by the verbs.

Note, therefore, that good instructional design has little to do with what is or is not "politically correct." We don't propose that teachers lecture less or use Socratic seminars simply because it is fashionable or progressive to say and do such things. Rather, it is the essence of the "if-then" logic of backward design: If your goal is student understanding and transfer, then you need to employ instructional methods aligned with these goals.

Design Task: Apply the ideas presented in Figures H.1 and H.2 to your Stage 3 planning. What ideas do you have for the teaching and learning needed to help students more effectively acquire, make meaning, and transfer?

Coding a Learning Plan

The A-M-T categories have proven useful as an analytic frame for reviewing a learning plan in light of these goals. In fact, a recommended use of the categories is to code your planned teaching and learning events in the Stage 3 plan using the letters A, M, and T (e.g., Is the teaching here primarily dedicated to helping students *acquire* basic information? Is this learning event mainly intended to help learners make *meaning* of a big idea?). Figure H.3 presents an example of such coding for units in science (physics), English/language arts (reading), and mathematics (linear equations).

Note: The A-M-T categories are not always "pure" in practice. A learning event that involves meaning (e.g., by having learners compare and contrast) may also enhance knowledge acquisition. Similarly, as learners attempt to transfer their learning, they often deepen their understanding (make meaning) of important principles. The purpose of the coding is simply to help designers clarify the *primary intent* of their planned teaching and learning events.

Design Task: Review your current Stage 3 and code the teaching and learning events using A-M-T (as in Figure H.3). Is there an appropriate balance? To what extent will your instruction appropriately address *all* of your Stage 1 goals? Revise your learning plan as needed following this analysis.

Figure H.1

A-M-T Learning Goals and Teaching Roles

Three Interrelated Learning Goals →	ACQUISITION	MEANING	TRANSFER
	This goal seeks to help learners *acquire* factual information and basic skills.	This goal seeks to help students *construct meaning* (i.e., *come to an understanding*) of important ideas and processes.	This goal seeks to support the learners' ability to *transfer* their learning autonomously and effectively in new situations.
Teacher Role and Instructional Strategies → *Note: Like the above learning goals, these three teaching roles (and their associated methods) work together in pursuit of identified learning results.*	**Direct Instruction** In this role, the primary role of teachers is to *inform* the learners through explicit instruction in targeted knowledge and skills; differentiating as needed. *Strategies include* • Lecture • Advance organizers • Graphic organizers • Questioning (convergent) • Demonstration/modeling • Process guides • Guided practice • Feedback, corrections • Differentiation	**Facilitative Teaching** Teachers in this role engage the learners in actively processing information and guide their inquiry into complex problems, texts, projects, cases, or simulations, differentiating as needed. *Strategies include* • Diagnostic assessment • Using analogies • Graphic organizers • Questioning (divergent) and probing • Concept attainment • Inquiry-oriented approaches • Problem-based learning • Socratic seminar • Reciprocal teaching • Formative (ongoing) assessments • Understanding notebook • Feedback/corrections • Rethinking and reflection prompts • Differentiated instruction	**Coaching** In a coaching role, teachers establish clear performance goals, supervise ongoing opportunities to perform (independent practice) in increasingly complex situations, provide models, and give ongoing feedback (as personalized as possible). They also provide just-in-time teaching (direct instruction) when needed. *Strategies include* • Ongoing assessment, providing specific feedback in the context of authentic application • Conferencing • Prompting self-assessment and reflection

⮕ **Design Tip:** Be careful! If you (or the textbook) merely provide students with prepackaged "meanings" (e.g., comparisons, critiques, interpretations, a summary) and simple step-by-step applications (e.g., tasks that require only "plug and chug," following directions), then this is *not* teaching for understanding, no matter how important the content or how accurate the summary!

Figure H.2

Action Verbs for A-M-T

Use these action verbs to help plan teaching and learning according to your A-M-T goals.

Goal Types	Action Verbs
Acquisition	• Apprehend • Calculate • Define • Discern • Identify • Memorize • Notice • Paraphrase • Plug in • Recall • Select • State
Meaning	• Analyze • Compare • Contrast • Critique • Defend • Evaluate • Explain • Generalize • Interpret • Justify/support • Prove • Summarize • Synthesize • Test • Translate • Verify
Transfer	• Adapt (based on feedback) • Adjust (based on results) • Apply • Create • Design • Innovate • Perform effectively • Self-assess • Solve • Troubleshoot

Figure H.3

Coding Learning Events Using A-M-T

After reviewing the examples below, try coding your learning events in terms of their primary intent—**A**cquisition, **M**eaning, or **T**ransfer of knowledge and skill.

Science—Physics

- Students observe four demonstrations of physical events (pendulum, pellet shooter, car slowing down, sling) and are asked to explain them in terms of the question "Why does that move the way it does?" **M**
- Students read the section in their physics textbook on the three laws of Newton and take a quiz on the content. **A**
- Students generalize from laboratory data related to cars going down inclined planes at varied heights and angles. **M**
- Students design a Rube Goldberg–type machine to illustrate principles of force, with specific reference to relevant Newtonian laws. **T**

English/Language Arts—Reading

- Students memorize words from a vocabulary list of those words. **A**
- Students make a web of the words' relationships and concepts. **M**
- Students group the words and consider, "What do these have in common?" **M**
- Students critique and edit a paper in which the new words are misused. **M**
- Students read a story containing the new words and explain their meaning in context. **T**
- Students use the recently learned words in various speaking and writing situations. **T**

Mathematics—Linear Equations

- Students study different graphs and data plots, and generalize about the patterns. **M**
- Students learn the formula $y = mx + b$ for linear equations. **A**
- Students solve practice problems using the formula to calculate slope. **A**
- Students compare linear and nonlinear relationships and explain the difference. **M**
- Students examine various real-world relationships (e.g., relationship of height to age, distance to speed, CD sales over time) and determine which ones are linear. **M**
- Students develop equations and graphic displays for representing relational data (with outliers and errors contained in the data). **T**

Coming to Understand

How, then, should we think about instruction that aims to develop understanding while also honoring our obligations to content? We can put it this way: our designs must involve not merely how content will be learned but how students will learn to think about and use it effectively. Content is a means, not the end. Thus we can take our two basic aspects of understanding and say that the aim in planning and teaching is that over time students will become increasingly better at (1) making meaning—drawing valid inferences using content and about content, and explaining the inferences in their own words; and (2) transfer—applying the content learned with increasing independence and effectiveness, in increasingly messy real-world contexts.

What must logically happen in the learning plan, then, to enable students to improve at these abilities over time? Before you think of teaching what must be "taught," think about providing the performance opportunities for developing those abilities—the tasks that require content understanding. In other words, you must "by design" ensure that there are

- Thought-provoking questions and challenges that require students to fit together the pieces of learning into generalizations.
- Opportunities for students to apply these generalizations in new (transfer) situations and to consider the feedback from attempts to do so (which may well lead to a modification of the original generalization).
- Experiences that show how knowledge and skill are building blocks to support meaning-making and transfer, not ends in themselves.

When teaching for understanding, it is important to recognize that an idea cannot just be taught and be expected to stick. An idea is a conclusion that students are helped to draw in the face of a need to make sense of content, not just another "fact" provided by teachers. It is an experience-induced theory, not a mere abstraction; it is a resultant generalization, not an obvious observation. Think of mystery movies or books: the reader is actively constructing an idea as to who is who, what their actions mean, and whodunit. So we don't really understand an idea if we haven't used it to make sense of things. Failure to help students actively make such meaning results in ideas that remain mere abstract and lifeless pieces of information. This teaching of ideas as if they were facts is also a primary cause of persistent student misconceptions and transfer deficits.

Making matters worse is that many students have come to expect all learning in school to be about acquisition and recall only. "Tell us what we need to know." "Is this going to be on the test?" Comments like these from older students are just one indicator that students have unfortunately become accustomed to thinking of learning as recall and regurgitation. (Unfortunately, their experience frequently makes this an *accurate* inference.)

What follows, then, for instruction generally when understanding is the goal yet students may be expecting all learning to involve acquisition only? Clearly, instruction must boldly signal that there are other aims besides acquisition.

Instruction for understanding thus best begins with and continually provides challenges to students' existing understanding of content, not the teaching of more content. Right from the start, learners must see that understanding demands active thought about what they know and can do, not simply an uncritical reception of new lessons. It must become clear to learners that understanding is not acquired but earned by proactive intellectual work: *What do I think this data/text/claim/set of facts/theory/art means? How can I find out if I am right? What do others think? Why do they think so? What, then?* Key inferences are not found in the text but in the thinking learner's mind.

So, what are some activities for achieving meaning? The following sections provide guidance and examples.

Developing Understanding Through Challenging Inquiry

You may know that many Japanese middle school math classes begin each new lesson with challenging problems rather than the teaching of new content. The aim is to make the new content appear needed after the learners have grappled with the challenges. Problem-based learning in science, in medical school, and in engineering is designed to accomplish the same end: help students understand the value of new learning while also giving them practice in constructing meaning and transferring knowledge to specific situations.

Imagine, then, beginning and framing a unit around inquiries, as in the following examples:

- "The title of our book is *Frog and Toad Are Friends*. But Frog tricks Toad into thinking it is May when it is really April! I am puzzled. Is that how friends really act toward one another? What's a *true* friend?"
- "Some people said we should drop the atomic bomb; others said we should have striven for peace, warned the Japanese, or not used the bomb. What's your view? How would you have advised Truman—knowing only what they knew then?"
- "Here are some data about women's marathon times. What is the trend? Are women likely to match the winning times for men in the marathon in the future?"
- "You know, I am stumped. I found this object [an owl pellet] near my home, and I don't know for sure what it is. What do *you* think it might be?" (Later: "What do we need to ask and investigate after we take it apart?")
- "Here is a video [in Spanish] of a scene in Madrid. What is going on here? What might you say to help the person in need, given your limited vocabulary?"

By regularly being confronted with such challenges and questions, learners become adept at tapping prior learning: *What does this remind me of? What have I learned about handling challenges of this sort? To what does this connect? How would I compare and contrast this to what we learned last week?* (The big ideas will be those points of connection.)

Here is a lengthier example of a unit on *Romeo and Juliet* that begins with questions:

Instead of just marching through the play, noting key scenes and issues, and quizzing students on the details, we ground the reading of the play in a set of important and valid questions—questions that will enable us to stay focused while we read the play and make it more likely that students will understand it. The questions are the following: Who "killed" Romeo and Juliet? What is true love? What role should adults play in the lives (and loves) of their children?

Before starting to read *Romeo and Juliet*, students respond to and discuss their answers to an "anticipation guide" survey based on these issues. Using a Likert scale for rating answers on a continuum, students respond to questions such as these: How much influence should parents have on who you go out with? Can young people find true love? Is love at first sight real or an illusion clouded by physical attraction? Through such initial inquiry and discussion—meaning-making activities all—students are now more ready to read the play proactively with specific helpful questions in mind, and likely to be more willing to acquire knowledge and skill related to the play.

As the reading of the play unfolds, students are asked to reconsider their initial "theories" about love, marriage, and family: "Have your views changed? Become clearer and more confident? Or questionable? Why?" This is the essence of facilitating meaning-making; that is, students develop their own theories and test them—against other theories, their own experience, and the facts (of the text, in this case)—while acquiring knowledge and skill in reading the play.

The final tasks should demand both meaning-making and transfer, too—and should be known *in advance* in order to focus student thinking and facilitate proactive meaning-making and transfer:

- In a mock trial, who should be tried and found "guilty" for the deaths of the lovers?
- What are guidelines for teenage love, based not only on our personal experience but on the wisdom of the play?
- How might the play be best restaged and written to communicate its universal ideas for modern ears and eyes?

Note that the content matters. Students have to engage in a close reading of the play, mindful of the questions, but the play is a *means* to greater understanding of timeless and meaningful inquiries. We read the play to better understand a human experience, and we test both the play's views and our own against one another. Along the way, we also teach students how to read more interpretively with an appreciation of the author's craft in using language.

Teaching Skills and Teaching for Understanding

Some teachers of mathematics (and other skill-focused areas, such as elementary reading and beginning foreign language) may think that the arguments made thus far do not apply to them: "Our job is to teach skills and ensure they are learned. We simply model the skill and then students just practice it." But the *intelligent* use of skill depends upon big ideas—underlying principles and strategic application. For instance, it's one thing to be a skilled dribbler in basketball; it's another to understand the principle of "creating space on offense" so that we "spread the court" when dribbling on a fast break.

The unit on statistics shown in Figure H.4 illustrates this point. The unit, designed for middle or high school statistics, focuses on measures of central tendency—mean, median, and mode. Although learning basic concepts and skills is certainly an aim, notice how this learning is framed by a broader inquiry, around essential questions: "What is 'fair'? To what extent can mathematics help us figure out 'fairness'?" Knowledge and skill acquisition (A) occurs in the context of meaning (M) and transfer (T). The math textbook helps us meet the acquisition goal, but the book does not address the meaning-making and transfer goals—that's where our design skills come in.

Review the key learning events in the unit plan (Figure H.4), coded using A-M-T. As you do, notice the sequence of the unit; for example, the use of the textbook to develop the basics comes after a challenging problem and related activities. Notice also that the unit culminates in a transfer task.

We can generalize from this and the previous examples. In a very real sense, *a unit focused on understanding is more about the larger questions and implications than the specific content.* To signal to students the priority of meaning-making and transfer, the unit must take them from the start through an inquiry with cycles of theorizing and testing along with simultaneous acquisition of knowledge and skill that is relevant to the inquiry. In brief, any unit plan might proceed roughly as follows:

- Introduce a question, problem, or other thought-provoking experience that challenges current understanding.
- Engender plausible different answers and disagreement among learners so that a more satisfactory "theory" is needed; do a K-W-L to set up what is known, what needs to be found out, and so on.
- Students either must develop their own theory or use ones provided by you, the text, or other students.
- Students try out their theory, refining ideas as needed and debating the merits of the different meanings.
- Students confront new challenges to their or the group's theory, provided by you, a text, a different experience, or some other new viewpoint.

- Students refine their ideas, as needed.
- Students transfer their theory to one or more concrete situations, as needed.
- Students generalize from their inquiries, being careful to note qualifications and nuances that derive from attempted transfer and discussions about the strengths, weaknesses, and limits of a theory.

Figure H.4

A-M-T for a Unit on Measures of Central Tendency

Essential Question: What is fair—and how can mathematics help us answer the question?

A = Acquiring basic knowledge and skills; **M** = Meaning; **T** = Transfer

1. Introduce and discuss the first part of the essential question: What is "fair"? What is "unfair"? **M**

2. Introduce a race problem: given the place of finish of all the runners in the four different grades from the high school, which class should be declared the fair winner in a whole-school run? Present a list that shows the grade level of each runner and the order in which he or she finished. The overall list of finishers is deliberately designed to make declaring a winner difficult: the mean should seem unfair, for example, age and gender might play a role. Students work in groups of four to propose the "fairest" solution and provide reasons for their approach. With the group work and presentations over, the teacher guides the class in a discussion in a summary of the issues raised. **M, T**

3. Teacher informs students about the broader mathematical connections at issue in the first two inquiries, and how those issues will be addressed by a consideration of measures of central tendency. The teacher lays out the unit activities in sequence and the culminating transfer and meaning-making tasks: Which approach to grading should be used in giving grades? What are the students' final reflections on the Essential Question about fairness and math? **A**

4. In small-group jigsaw, students share their answers, then return to their team to generalize from all the small-group work. Discuss other examples related to the concept of "fairness," such as the following: **M**

- What is a fair way to rank many teams when they do not all play each other?

- What is a fair way to split up limited food among hungry people of different sizes?

- When is it "fair" to use majority vote and when is it not fair? What might be more fair?

- Is it fair to have apportioned representatives based on a state's population, yet have two senators from each state irrespective of the state's size? What might be more fair?

- What are fair and unfair ways of representing how much money the "average" worker earns, for purposes of making government policy?

5. Teacher connects the discussion to the next section in the textbook—measures of central tendency (mean, median, mode, range, standard deviation). **A**

6. Students practice calculating each type of measure. **A**

7. Teacher gives quiz on mean, median, mode from textbook. **A**

8. Teacher leads a review and discussion of the quiz results. **A M**

9. Group task worked on in class: What is the fairest possible grading system for schools to use? **M T**

10. Individuals and small teams present their grading policy recommendations and reasons. **M T**

11. Culminating transfer task: Each student determines which measure (mean, median, or mode) should be used to calculate his or her grade for the marking period and writes a note to the teacher showing the calculations used and explaining the choice. **T**

12. Students write a reflection on the essential question. **M T**

Learning to Transfer

As the examples suggest, focused inquiry promotes the goal of transfer. The research is very clear on this point: students who really develop and "own" an idea are more likely to successfully interpret new situations and tackle new problems than students who possess only drilled knowledge and skill.

> The first object of any act of learning... is that it should serve us in the future.... In essence, it consists in learning initially not a skill but a general idea which can then be used as a basis for recognizing subsequent problems.... This type of transfer is at the heart of the educational process—the continual broadening and deepening of knowledge in terms of... ideas. (Bruner, 1960, p. 17)

> A key finding is that organizing information into a conceptual framework allows for greater transfer.... The research clearly shows that usable knowledge is not the same as a mere list of disconnected facts. Expert knowledge is connected and organized around important concepts; it is conditionalized by context; it supports understanding and transfer to other contexts. (Bransford Brown, & Cocking, 2000, p. 9)

> Students develop flexible understanding of when, where, why, and how to use their knowledge to solve new problems if they learn how to extract underlying principles and themes from their learning exercises. (Bransford et al., 2000, p. 224)

The units on statistics and *Romeo and Juliet* illustrate the importance of powerful ideas and consideration of context in transfer. The final tasks can be done well only by thinking carefully about fairness and love, and by bringing in personal experience and prior learning to a very specific context for the tasks at hand.

As the mathematics example also indicates, a key element in transfer is that the student is challenged to apply learning to a new and specific setting in which sensitivity to context (as well as fidelity to the original knowledge) matters. Rote learning or drill and practice alone can never prepare students for such transfer. This point directly relates to high-stakes accountability testing. Our analysis of standardized test results from states that publish their tests and the results reveals that the most challenging (i.e., widely missed) items on standardized tests are *not* questions requiring recall or basic skills (Wiggins, 2010). They invariably involve transfer because the readings, writing prompts, and word problems encountered are all new or unfamiliar looking. Thus the best way to prepare for tests in the long run is to teach for understanding and transfer, with discrete knowledge and skill learned in the context of meaningful inquiry and contextualized application. We now summarize the research on transfer so that designers can consider how best to develop learners' ability to increasingly apply learning on their own, in flexible and context-sensitive ways:

- *Establish and keep highlighting clear transfer goals.* Explicitly and regularly alert learners to the goal of transfer. Why? Because most students do not realize that this is the goal of learning. They are quite convinced—from prior experience and, especially, typical tests—that the aim is to recall and plug in what was previously taught. Make clear that the "transfer" game is very different from the "recall and plug in" game.

  Initially, make this clear through think-alouds and explicit reminders of what you and your students are now doing and what its purpose is. Spend time going over the kinds of transfer performance they will need to be able to do well by the end of the unit or course. For example, "By the end of the unit, you'll have to do this product on your own, with no prompts or cues from me. Here are a few model student papers from past years, and a rubric describing the end goal." Or "Initially, you will just mimic some approaches I teach you. But later you will have to invent your own approach or adapt one you have learned to a new task."

- *Have learners practice judgment in using a few different skills, not just plugging in one skill on command.* Transfer is about judging *which* skill and knowledge to use *when.* Transfer is thus about smart strategy in the use of a repertoire of skills. (Psychologists refer to this as "conditional" knowledge as opposed to "declarative" and "procedural" knowledge). Make sure learners have the opportunity to hear think-alouds of your own problem solving or text interpreting. Give students practice and get feedback on their attempts to judge which skill or knowledge might be best in a particular situation. Have learners do think-alouds and report on why they did what they did when they did it. Learning to self-monitor in this way improves both self-assessment and self-adjustment.

- *Provide students with feedback (without grading) on their self-cueing, knowledge retrieval, self-assessment, and self-adjustment.* As in sports and independent reading, students need countless opportunities to self-prompt, self-assess, and self-adjust—with teacher feedback on the attempts. What does the student do when you *don't* supply the graphic organizers or a big hint that they should use the writing technique they studied yesterday? Unfortunately, the research is clear: many students do not self-prompt, in the absence of explicit direction. "You didn't say to use it!" is a common and unfortunate comment. So it's important to constantly "test" (without necessarily evaluating them or entering the grade in the grade book) students' ability to self-cue. For example, give them unfamiliar-looking items, writing prompts, or problems with no mention of which knowledge is being tapped and which strategies and tools they should use. See what they do on their own, then go over the assessment carefully in class soon after. Debrief like a coach: What kind of task did they think it was? Why didn't they think to use Graphic Organizer X or Strategy Y, since it should have seemed so clearly related to the task?

- *Change the set up so that students realize that use of prior learning comes in many guises.* The research on transfer stresses that students need to be given tasks in which the setting/format/context/mode/language is sufficiently varied over time that students learn they have to think more flexibly in tapping their knowledge. The student too often thinks—and wishes!—that a recipe or plug-in formula will solve all future needs. Make clear that the initial recipe or structure or scaffold is just that—a scaffold or crutch to be eventually replaced by fluid decision making. Too often students work too rigidly or mechanically in applying their learning, rather than seeing application as use of an *idea*. For example, teach the five-paragraph essay, the three-paragraph essay, and the no-paragraph argument (i.e., a powerful advertisement). Make clear that the transfer goal is "rational persuasion," not simply using a one-size-fits-all strategy like 'the five-paragraph essay.' Give students increasingly odd "looks" at a task or a problem that requires the same knowledge (e.g., increasingly nonroutine and unobvious problems involving the Pythagorean theorem).

- *Have students regularly generalize from specific (and increasingly challenging) instances and cases.* Transfer is about using helpful big ideas to find familiarities and connections where others see only newness and difference. Ask students to generalize from their experience and immediate past lessons to more widely applicable principles, rules, and ideas. For example, after studying westward expansion, ask, "What big ideas about human migration does the pioneer movement west suggest? Can you support your generalizations using other evidence?" Then ask the same question after studying early 20th century immigration, and help them understand that this kind of transfer will be more and more requested of them on their own—using ideas to see connections and transfer.

- *Require students to constantly reword/rephrase/re-present what they learn.* Whether by just taking notes or creatively placing a complete text in a new genre, time, and place, making learners recast what they have learned in their own terms is a significant aid to long-term memory and flexible use of knowledge, according to the research on learning and transfer.

This discussion of teaching for meaning and transfer should also sensitize you to two common mistakes in planning and teaching: too much didactic teaching and too little. We teach too much when we treat all our goals as being exclusively knowledge and skill, capable of being "apprehended" via one-shot coverage. Coverage in the bad sense is really the illusion of "teaching by mentioning"—as if hearing everything of value and practicing discrete skills a few times can make you never forget your learning and make you understand and be able to wisely use everything you are taught.

The other extreme—teaching too little—errs in the opposite direction by treating all learning as "learning by discovery." That approach is a mistake on three counts. First, it ignores that an important body of knowledge, skill, and strategy needs to be explicitly modeled, taught, and learned—and that the research on learning is unequivocal about the need for direct and guided instruction. Second, it overlooks the fact that most big ideas are not obvious and often at odds with common sense. Finally, it improperly assumes that understanding will just somehow happen (and therefore, by extension, that *any* meaning or performance that strikes the student's fancy is OK). In other words, the teacher has to be an active facilitator and coach of meaning-making and transfer if genuine student understanding is to eventually occur "by design" instead of "by luck."

The Role of the Textbook

As we warned in earlier modules, a textbook may be necessary but is usually not sufficient as a full course of study. It is best viewed as a resource for knowledge and skill development, organized by topics to suit a generic audience all over the country. The assessments rarely ask for meaning-making and transfer. It is thus imperative that teachers design a course of study and appropriate units to frame the use of the textbook around long-term understanding goals. What does your textbook contain or not contain, given your understanding-related goals?

The Need to Cue Students into A-M-T

Students rarely understand until it is far too late in their school career that meaning-making and transfer are the primary goals of education. They too often grow up thinking that their only job is acquisition of knowledge and skill. Aided and abetted by too much content coverage and test prep, students come to see learning as simply knowing the answer and being ready to give it back on the test. As one of our students once said, "Enough of this discussion; just tell us what the story means!" Teachers of mathematics have also told us that some students and parents complain when a test presents a new problem to solve (i.e., "We didn't study that specific problem in that form—it's unfair!"). Such comments indicate that at least some students (and parents) may not understand that meaning-making and transfer are the key goals of education, and that not all learning is acquisition.

It is thus imperative that teachers carefully and explicitly help students understand that there are different learning goals—A-M-T—that require different strategies for which there will be different kinds of assessments. This can be done through written syllabi, letters home, commentaries on tests from prior years posted on websites, and other means.

In conclusion, we invite you to revisit your draft learning plan in light of the three goals—acquisition, meaning-making, and transfer—and the instructional approaches suggested in this module.

Self-Assessment—Review Criteria for Module H

Review your current unit sketch against the following criteria:

- Are all three learning goal types (acquisition, meaning, transfer) addressed in my draft learning plan?
- Have I sketched out learning events that are appropriate for each type of goal, rather than what is merely most familiar or comfortable?
- Are there sufficient opportunities for students to draw inferences and make meaning on their own about the big ideas of the unit?
- Have I sketched out a flow of the unit that gradually releases students to be more responsible for figuring out what to do and when to do it?

The Nutrition Unit Revisited

Figure H.5 shows the Stage 3 learning events coded as *A*, *M*, or *T*. This coding enables designers to check to see that all three goals—acquisition, meaning, and transfer—are all properly addressed in the learning plan.

Online you'll find two helpful worksheets: Figure H.6, Learning for Understanding (A-M-T) and Figure H.7, Using the Textbook Wisely. Both provide templates and prompts for planning learning events.

Further Information on the Ideas and Issues in This Module

How People Learn (Bransford, Brown, & Cocking, 2000).

The Paideia Proposal (Adler, 1982).

Schooling by Design: Mission, Action, and Achievement (Wiggins & McTighe, 2007). Chapter 4.

Understanding by Design: Professional Development Workbook (McTighe & Wiggins, 2004). Page 118.

References

Adler, M. (1982). *The Paideia proposal: An educational manifesto*. New York: Macmillan.

Bloom, B. (Ed.). (1956). *Taxonomy of educational objectives, handbook 1: Cognitive domain*. Chicago: University of Chicago Press.

Bransford, J., Brown, A., & Cocking, R. (Eds.). (2000). *How people learn: Brain, mind, experience, and school* (Expanded ed.). Washington, DC: National Academy Press.

Bruner, J. (1960). *The process of education.* Cambridge, MA: Harvard University Press.

McTighe, J., & Wiggins, G. (2004). *Understanding by design: Professional development workbook.* Alexandria, VA: ASCD.

Wiggins, G. (2010, March). Why we should stop bashing state tests. *Educational Leadership, 67*(6), 48–52.

Wiggins, G., & McTighe, J. (2005). *Understanding by design* (2nd ed.). Alexandria, VA: ASCD.

Wiggins, G., & McTighe, J. (2007). *Schooling by design: Mission, action, and achievement.* Alexandria, VA: ASCD.

Figure H.5

Nutrition Unit, Stage 3: Coded Learning Events Using A-M-T

A = Acquiring basic knowledge and skills

M = Making meaning

T = Transfer

1. Begin with an entry question (*Can the foods you eat cause zits?*) to hook students into considering the effects of nutrition on their lives. **M**

2. Introduce the essential questions and discuss the culminating unit performance tasks (Chow Down and Eating Action Plan). **M**

3. Note: Key vocabulary terms are introduced as needed by the various learning activities and performance tasks. Students read and discuss relevant selections from the health textbook to support the learning activities and tasks. As an ongoing activity students keep a chart of their daily eating and drinking for later review and evaluation. **A**

4. Present concept attainment lesson on the food groups. Then have students practice categorizing pictures of foods accordingly. **M**

5. Introduce the Food Pyramid and identify foods in each group. Students work in groups to develop a poster of the Food Pyramid containing cut-out pictures of foods in each group. Display the posters in the classroom or hallway. **A**

6. Give a quiz on the food groups and Food Pyramid (matching format). **A**

7. Review and discuss the nutrition brochure from the USDA. Discussion question: *Must everyone follow the same diet in order to be healthy?* **A M**

8. Working in cooperative groups, students analyze a hypothetical family's diet (deliberately unbalanced) and make recommendations for improved nutrition. Teacher observes and coaches students as they work. **M T**

9. Have groups share their diet analyses and discuss as a class. **M**

(Note: Teacher collects and reviews the diet analyses to look for misunderstandings needing instructional attention.)

10. Each student designs an illustrated nutrition brochure to teach younger children about the importance of good nutrition for healthy living and the problems associated with poor eating. This activity is completed outside class. **M T**

11. Show and discuss the video *Nutrition and You*. Discuss the health problems linked to poor eating. **A**

12. Students listen to, and question, a guest speaker (nutritionist from the local hospital) about health problems caused by poor nutrition. **A**

13. Students respond to written prompt: *Describe two health problems that could arise as a result of poor nutrition, and explain what changes in eating could help to avoid them.* (These are collected and graded by teacher.) **A**

14. Teacher models how to read and interpret food label information on nutritional values. Then students practice using donated boxes, cans, and bottles (empty!). **A**

15. Students work independently to develop the three-day camp menu. **T**

16. At the conclusion of the unit, students review their completed daily eating chart and self-assess the healthfulness of their eating. Have they noticed changes? Improvements? Do they notice changes in how they feel or their appearance? **M T**

17. Students develop a personal "eating action plan" for healthful eating. These are saved and presented at upcoming student-involved parent conferences. **T**

18. Conclude the unit with student self-evaluation regarding their personal eating habits. Each student develops a personal action plan for his or her "healthful eating" goal. **M T**

Afterword

Over the course of this Design Guide, you have learned how to use the updated UbD Template, version 2.0, to plan curriculum units "backward" from understanding-related goals.

You have worked through the three stages to create a draft unit that includes the following elements:

Stage 1
- Transfer Goals
- Essential Questions and Understandings
- Knowledge and Skill Objectives
- Relevant Standards and Other Established Goals

Stage 2
- Performance Tasks and Other Evidence
- Evaluative Criteria

Stage 3
- An outline of the Learning Plan emphasizing Meaning-Making and Transfer

If this is your first time planning with UbD, you may have found the process demanding, and perhaps even a bit uncomfortable. Many beginners have observed that while the logic of backward design makes sense, the actual design process is more difficult than they imagined. The good news is that with practice, backward design becomes more natural; indeed, it becomes a way of thinking. If you approached the *Guide* with some experience in UbD, we trust that your understanding of it has deepened and that you are more confident in transferring this approach when designing units. Finally, we trust that you see the power in the new template—even if it means a change in routine.

We hope that you will continue your UbD learning with other available products as we continue to explore and expand the resources based on the experiences of thousands of educators worldwide. We will continue to upload UbD resources to the dedicated page for the UbD group on ASCD EDge. Go to http://groups.ascd.org/groups/detail/110884/understanding-by-design/.

About the Authors

 **Grant Wiggins** is president of Authentic Education in Hopewell, New Jersey. He earned his EdD from Harvard University and his BA from St. John's College in Annapolis. Grant and his colleagues consult with schools, districts, and state and national education departments on a variety of reform matters. He and his colleagues also organize conferences and workshops, and develop print and web resources on key school reform issues.

Grant is perhaps best known for being coauthor, with Jay McTighe, of *Understanding by Design*, the award-winning and highly successful program and set of materials on curriculum design used all over the world, and of *Schooling by Design*. He is also a coauthor for Pearson Publishing on more than a dozen textbook programs in which UbD is infused. His work has been supported by the Pew Charitable Trusts, the Geraldine R. Dodge Foundation, and the National Science Foundation.

For 25 years, Grant has worked on influential reform initiatives around the world, including Ted Sizer's Coalition of Essential Schools; the International Baccalaureate Program; the Advanced Placement Program; state reform initiatives in New Jersey, New York, and Delaware; and national reforms in China, the Philippines, and Thailand.

Grant is widely known for his work in assessment reform. He is the author of *Educative Assessment* and *Assessing Student Performance*, both published by Jossey-Bass. He was a lead consultant on many state assessment reform initiatives, such as the portfolio project in Vermont and performance assessment consortia in New Jersey and North Carolina.

Several journals have published Grant's articles, including *Educational Leadership* and *Phi Delta Kappan*. His work is grounded in 14 years of secondary school teaching and coaching. Grant taught English and electives in philosophy, coached varsity soccer and cross country, as well as junior varsity baseball and track and field. He also plays in the Hazbins, a rock band. Grant may be contacted at grant@authenticeducation.org.

 **Jay McTighe** brings a wealth of experience developed during a rich and varied career in education. He served as director of the Maryland Assessment Consortium, a state collaboration of school districts working together to develop and share formative performance assessments. Prior to this position, Jay was involved with school improvement projects at the Maryland State Department of Education where he directed the development of the Instructional Framework, a multimedia database on teaching. Jay is well known for his work with thinking skills, having coordinated statewide efforts to develop instructional strategies, curriculum models, and assessment procedures for improving the quality of student thinking. In addition to his work at the state level, Jay has experience at the district level in Prince George's County, Maryland, as a classroom teacher, resource specialist, and program coordinator. He also directed a state residential enrichment program for gifted and talented students.

Jay is an accomplished author, having coauthored 10 books, including the best-selling *Understanding by Design* series with Grant Wiggins. He has written more than 30 articles and book chapters, and has published in leading journals, including *Educational Leadership* (ASCD) and *The Developer* (National Staff Development Council).

Jay has an extensive background in professional development and is a regular speaker at national, state, and district conferences and workshops. He has made presentations in 47 states within the United States, in 7 Canadian provinces, and 18 other countries on 5 continents.

Jay received his undergraduate degree from the College of William and Mary, earned his master's degree from the University of Maryland, and completed postgraduate studies at the Johns Hopkins University. He was selected to participate in the Educational Policy Fellowship Program through the Institute for Educational Leadership in Washington, D.C., and served as a member of the National Assessment Forum, a coalition of education and civil rights organizations advocating reforms in national, state, and local assessment policies and practices. Contact information: Jay McTighe, 6581 River Run, Columbia, MD 21044-6066 USA. E-mail: jmctigh@aol.com.